Arguments:

Deductive Logic
Exercises

Arguments:

Deductive Logic
Exercises

Howard Pospesel
University of Miami

Prentice-Hall, Inc.
Englewood Cliffs, New Jersey

To all and only those persons
to whom no books
are ever dedicated.

Cover photo by Rocky Walters.

13–045963–1

Library of Congress Catalog Card No.: 76–125840

Current printing (last number):
10 9 8 7 6 5 4

Printed in the United States of America

Prentice-Hall International, Inc., London
Prentice-Hall of Australia, Pty. Ltd., Sydney
Prentice-Hall of Canada, Ltd., Toronto
Prentice-Hall of India Private Limited, New Delhi
Prentice-Hall of Japan, Inc., Tokyo

Student's Preface

On the following pages you will find arguments treating such diverse topics as "pot," the existence of God, the morality of manufacturing napalm, and the nature of mathematics.* I have had a great time formulating these arguments; I hope you will enjoy analyzing them. I also hope that as you work through this set of exercises you will become more aware of the arguments encountered in your other reading and of those you advance in conversation and writing.

One word of warning is pertinent. In order for an argument to establish the truth of its conclusion it must possess *two* virtues— a valid form and true premises. Some of the arguments in this volume contain false premises. Hence, merely from the fact that an argument in this collection exhibits a valid form it does not follow that its conclusion is true. This caution is particularly important in connection with arguments dealing with philosophical issues. They should be regarded as *starting* philosophical discussions, rather than as conclusively *ending* discussion.

Several conventions which have been adopted require explanation. (1) In sections two and three capital letters represent affirmative, rather than negative, sentences. For example, if R is used in symbolizing 'It is not raining,' it will represent the affirmative sentence 'It is raining.' The longer sentence will be symbolized by using R with the negation sign.

(2) In the second and third sections, premises and conclusions which are simple sentences (or the negations of simple sen-

---

* Arguments 350, 156–159, 392–394, and 232–234, respectively.

v

tences) are often followed by capital letters enclosed in parentheses. Such a letter is to be used to represent the sentence (or, in the case of a negative sentence, the affirmative portion of the sentence) which precedes it.

(3) Some sentences in sections two through seven begin with the expression 'If this is so (true, correct).' The word 'this' refers to the immediately preceding sentence.

(4) The notion of "universe of discourse" is employed in sections four through seven. The universe of discourse is simply the class of objects one is considering in a given context. Using a universe of discourse often simplifies the analysis of an argument. To illustrate the idea: Suppose an argument contains as a premise 'Every male cat hates every other male cat.' If the argument is concerned exclusively with cats, we are free to adopt the class of cats as our universe of discourse. Having done so we symbolize the premise mentioned above as if it read "Every male hates every other male."

(5) Throughout the book these expressions are used interchangeably:

> The inference from P to Q is *valid*.
> P *entails* Q.
> P *logically implies* Q.
> Q *follows logically* from P.

(6) Numerals used in cross-references indicate arguments rather than pages.

I am indebted to Ray Bielec, Douglas Browning, Hon-Fai Lee, David Marans, and Fred Westphal for suggesting problems; to Max Black and David Marans for reading and criticizing the manuscript; to Rocky Walters for engaging in syllogistic arguments with policemen; to my wife, Carmen, for advice on style; and to my children, Michael, Amy, and Mark, whose orneriness kept me at school working on this volume.

Teacher's Preface

This set of five hundred deductive arguments is intended to be used as a companion for a logic textbook. Since the book uses no logic symbols and employs no specific logical techniques it is compatible with any logic text. The need for *Arguments* stems from the fact that almost every logic book suffers from one or both of the following defects: an insufficient number of sample arguments, and insignificant, contrived, and uninteresting arguments. When a student encounters only exercises of the "If Alice marries Bob, Sue will be maid of honor" variety, he must wonder whether logic has any utility. I have tried to provide in this volume nonartificial arguments with significant conclusions. Work on these arguments will provide the student with practice in symbolizing and in employing tests of validity. More exercises have been included than would typically be used in a semester course so that fresh problems can be assigned in succeeding semesters. While this book is intended to supplement a text, its use would enable a teacher to substitute his lectures for a textbook.

The exercises are divided into four main classes. The first three correspond to commonly treated branches of logic: syllogistic, truth-functional, and quantificational logic. The set of syllogisms (section one) concludes with some sorites. The truth-functional arguments (sections two and three) are divided into two groups. The first contains a mixture of valid and invalid arguments which are suitable for truth-table analysis. No problem in this set contains more than four atomic statements, and most contain fewer. The second group of truth-functional arguments is restricted to valid inferences and is designed for practice in constructing deductions. The quantificational arguments (sections four through seven) are split into two groups: those involving only *monadic* predicates and those containing *relational* predicates. This division accommodates teachers who do not wish to discuss relations. Each of these two groups is subdivided into a set of valid arguments (for deduction practice) and a set of mixed valid and invalid ones (for practicing invalidity proofs). In each of sections two through seven arguments are ordered (roughly) by difficulty. Arguments clearly beyond the abilities of introductory students appear only at the ends of sections and are marked "DIFFICULT."

The final group (section eight) consists of arguments as they appeared in newspapers, magazines, journals, and books. It is hoped that a consideration of these passages will help the student to spot and evaluate arguments encountered in his own reading. The relational arguments in section eight are relegated to the back.

Section one can also be used with quantificational techniques, and this section together with four and five will provide practice for a study of class logic.

Table
of Contents

Arguments:

Deductive Logic
Exercises

1 Valid and Invalid Syllogistic Arguments

1. Five Miami police cars responded to a complaint that a girl in Bayfront Park was indecently attired. One policeman drove his cruiser onto the grass in spite of a sign reading "NO CARS OR TRUCKS OF ANY KIND ALLOWED IN PARK." When a philosophy graduate student, Rocky Walters, complained to the policeman, the latter contended that the sign did not apply to his cruiser. Rocky advanced the following argument, but the policeman was unmoved.

No cars are allowed in the park. Police cruisers are cars. Therefore police cruisers are not allowed in the park.

(C = cars, V = vehicles allowed in the park, P = police cruisers)

2. Is our behavior caused (in part) by our motives? One could use argument 2 to support a negative answer to this question.

Causes are events. Motives aren't events. So motives aren't causes.

(C, E, M)

1

3. Any man who had a definite set of rules of conduct by which he regulated his life would be a machine. There is no man who has such a set of rules. Therefore no men are machines.[1]

(A = men who have definite sets of rules of conduct by which they regulate their lives, B = machines, C = men)

4. There are valid arguments which contain one or more false premises. This proves that some valid arguments do not establish their conclusions, because no argument which has one or more false premises establishes its conclusion.

(V = valid arguments, F = arguments containing one or more false premises, E = arguments which establish their conclusions)

5. No teacher who is in the military has academic freedom. So ROTC instructors lack academic freedom, since they are all teachers who are in the military.

(M = teachers who are members of the military, F = persons who have academic freedom, R = ROTC instructors)

6. Professional boxing should pass out of existence, because most professional boxers are severely and permanently injured as a result of boxing, and any sport which seriously and permanently injures most of its participants should cease to exist.

(B = sports identical to professional boxing, P = sports which should pass from existence, I = sports which severely and permanently injure most of their participants)

7. At least one a priori proposition is not vacuous. This is a con-

---

[1] This argument is discussed (but not advanced) by A. M. Turing in "Computing Machinery and Intelligence," *Mind,* LIX (1950), 452.

sequence of the following facts: (1) each analytic proposition is vacuous, and (2) there are a priori propositions which are not analytic.

($B =$ a priori propositions, $V =$ vacuous propositions, $C =$ analytic propositions)

8.   A good library is a *sine qua non* for greatness in a university. Duke has a good library. Hence it must be a great university.

($L =$ universities having good libraries, $G =$ great universities, $D =$ universities identical to Duke)

9. When a Miami concert by the Doors got out of control, with members of the audience milling about on the stage, the concert promoter grabbed the microphone and said, "Only musicians are permitted on the stage." The group's singer, Jim Morrison shouted, "You're not a musician," and pushed the promoter off the stage into the audience. Obviously Morrison was advancing an argument with an unstated conclusion, namely, 'You're not permitted on the stage.' Evaluate the argument. ($M =$ musicians, $S =$ persons permitted on the stage, $Y =$ persons identical to the promoter)

10. Some philosophers maintain that all meaningful words are names. It is of some interest to refute this false thesis, since it has been used as a basis for metaphysical theorizing. Argument 10 is one simple criticism of it.[2]

          All prepositions are meaningful. No prepositions are names. Therefore it is false that all meaningful words are names.

($P, M =$ meaningful terms, N)

---

[2] Other criticisms are given in 176, 283, and 321.

11. Philosophers who accept the thesis mentioned in the preceding exercise may use it to support the claim that general nouns (like 'cow') and adjectives (like 'green') are names. Their reasoning is represented by argument 11. Having established to their satisfaction that general nouns and adjectives are names, they maintain that these terms name "universals" (entities which are purportedly real even though they do not occupy space or time).

> All meaningful words are names. Since general nouns and adjectives are meaningful, they must be names.

$(M, N, G =$ general nouns and adjectives)

12. No argument whose premises are logically contradictory establishes its conclusion. This is a consequence of the following facts: (1) every argument with a logically contradictory premise set contains at least one false premise; (2) no argument which contains one or more false premises establishes its conclusion.

$(L =$ arguments with logically contradictory premise sets, $E =$ arguments which establish their conclusions, $F =$ arguments containing at least one false premise)

13. The headline on an advertisement for Nicholson files runs "If you never use a file, you don't need this book." Then follows the sentence "But we're pretty sure you do, so we're offering FILE FILOSOPHY, free, to anyone who fills in the coupon." [3] The ad seems to be advancing argument 13.

> Persons who do not use files do not need this book. You are a person who uses files. So you need this book.

----

[3] *Popular Science Monthly*, February, 1965, p. 198.

(F = persons who use files, B = persons who need this book, Y = persons identical to you)

14.   Since not all acts of civil disobedience are violent and many nonviolent acts are morally justified, at least some civil-disobedient actions are justified from the moral standpoint.

(C = civil-disobedient acts, V = violent acts, M = morally justified acts)

15. In *The Principles of Human Knowledge*,[4] George Berkeley notes that the philosopher Locke reasons from the fact that brutes (that is, nonhuman animals) do not use words to the conclusion that they do not have the ability to form abstract general ideas. Berkeley claims that the suppressed premise in this inference is 'the making use of words implies the having general ideas.' Is Berkeley right? Put another way, is 15 valid?

Brutes do not use words. All who use words have abstract general ideas. Hence brutes do not have abstract general ideas.

(B = brutes, W = word-users, A = those who have abstract general ideas)

16. State Mutual of America offers life insurance at reduced rates to nonsmokers. They give this explanation in a magazine ad:

You see, we're convinced that people who don't smoke cigarettes are better risks than people who do. And better risks deserve better rates.[5]

---

[4] *A Treatise Concerning the Principles of Human Knowledge*, pp. 10–11. (The facts of publication are given in the bibliography.)
[5] *Newsweek*, February 17, 1969, p. 101.

This explanation is syllogistic. The unstated conclusion is 'Non-smokers deserve better rates.' (N = nonsmokers, R = better risks, D = persons who deserve better rates)

17.　　　　Nobody under forty is a World War Two veteran. There are no veterans of World War Two in the undergraduate student body. It follows that every undergraduate is under forty.

(F = persons under forty, V = veterans of World War Two, U = undergraduates)

18. Associated Press news item:

> Augusta, Maine—A bill in the state legislature reads: "Every person residing in Maine who earns less than $4,000 annually shall be furnished a hearing aid free of charge by the Department of Health and Welfare."
> Rep. Robert Soulas of Bangor said, "I guess this bill needs some work" when he was told his measure didn't say you had to be hard of hearing.[6]

The bill's defect is made explicit by this syllogism:

> Every person residing in Maine who earns less than $4,000 annually shall be furnished a hearing aid free of charge by the Department of Health and Welfare. Some Maine residents earning less than $4,000 per year are not hard of hearing. Therefore some persons to whom the Department of Health and Welfare will supply free hearing aids are not hard of hearing.

(M = Maine residents earning less than $4,000 annually, F = per-

[6] "Maine Bill Needs to Be Polished Up" (Associated Press), *The Miami News*, March 10, 1969, p. 6–A.

sons who will be furnished free hearing aids by the Department of Health and Welfare, H = persons who are hard of hearing)

19. No one who knowingly and needlessly endangers his health is rational. Every college student who smokes is knowingly and unnecessarily endangering his health. It follows that college students who smoke aren't rational.

(H = persons who knowingly and needlessly endanger their health, R = rational persons, S = college students who smoke)

20. In *A History of Western Philosophy*, Bertrand Russell writes:

All the important inferences outside logic and pure mathematics are inductive, not deductive; the only exceptions are law and theology, each of which derives its first principles from an unquestionable text, viz. the statute books or the scriptures.[7]

One could attack Russell's thesis as follows:

At least some philosophical arguments are important inferences which are outside the areas of logic, mathematics, law, and theology. At least some inferences in philosophy are not inductive. Thus it is false that all important inferences outside of logic, mathematics, law, and theology are inductive.

(P = philosophical inferences, O = important inferences outside of logic, mathematics, law, and theology, I = inductive inferences)

21. Any reason for rejecting mind-body dualism is also a reason for rejecting the view that the human soul survives the death of the body. The difficulty of explaining how two such different

---

[7] P. 199.

substances as mind and body could interact is a reason for repudiating dualism. Consequently it is also a reason for refusing to accept the soul-survival thesis.

Mind-body dualism is the view that each human is composed of two distinct substances: a physical body, and a nonphysical mind or soul. Note that 21 does not count against the view that the human *body* will be resurrected. (*D* = reasons for rejecting mind-body dualism, *S* = reasons for rejecting the view that the soul survives the death of the body, *I* = reasons identical to the one concerning how difficult it is to explain mind-body interaction)

22. All syllogisms which have two universal premises and a particular conclusion are invalid.[8] Every syllogism which has two "A" premises and an "I" conclusion is a syllogism with two universal premises and a particular conclusion. Hence some syllogisms with two "A" premises and an "I" conclusion are invalid.

(*U* = syllogisms with two universal premises and a particular conclusion, *I* = invalid syllogisms, *A* = syllogisms with two "A" premises and an "I" conclusion)

23. Kant argues in *Foundations of the Metaphysics of Morals*:[9]

No adequate study of ethics will be empirical; because any adequate ethical study will yield principles which apply universally and with necessity, but no empirical study yields such principles.

(*A* = adequate studies of ethics, *E* = empirical studies, *P* = studies which yield principles which apply universally and with necessity)

---

[8] This premise is debatable.
[9] Pp. 24–25. Argument 142 is another Kantian attack on the empirical approach to ethics.

24.　　　Conclusive proof that the earth is spherical is provided by these two observations: (1) spheres cast curved shadows; and (2) the earth casts a curved shadow (on the moon during a lunar eclipse).

(E = planets identical to the earth, S = spheres, C = objects which cast curved shadows)

25. According to the philosopher J. L. Watling, Descartes held that any true proposition can be known on the basis of understanding alone.[10] Watling's criticism of this thesis is summarized by 25.

Any proposition which can be known on the basis of understanding alone is logically true. There are true propositions which are not logically true. So it is false that all true propositions can be known merely on the basis of understanding them.

(K = propositions which can be known on the basis of understanding alone, L = logically true propositions, T = true propositions)

26.　　　A person who makes Pascal's wager is adopting a calculating and self-regarding attitude toward God. God is not pleased by persons who adopt such an attitude. It follows that God is not happy with people who make Pascal's wager.[11]

See 103 for an account of Pascal's wager. (W = persons who make Pascal's wager, A = persons who adopt a calculating attitude toward God, P = persons who please God)

---

[10] "Descartes," in A Critical History of Western Philosophy, ed. by D. J. O'Connor, p. 172.
[11] This argument is advanced by John Hick, Philosophy of Religion, p. 64.

27.   Every argument in mathematics is deductive. Most mathematical arguments are not syllogistic. This proves that some deductive arguments are not syllogisms.[12]

(M = mathematical arguments, D = deductive arguments, S = syllogisms)

28.   Being a tautology is a sufficient condition for being a formal truth. Each formal truth is a logical truth. Hence there are no nontautologous logical truths.

(T = tautologies, F = formal truths, L = logical truths)

29. The *instrumentalist* in philosophy of science denies that the sentences in scientific theories have truth values. One of his arguments for this position is summed up by 29.

        The sentences of theory are rules. Since rules are neither true nor false, theoretical sentences aren't either true or false.

(T = theoretical sentences, R = rules, A = sentences which are either true or false)

30. News item:

        CHEYENNE, Wyo.—The Wyoming Senate amended a proposed constitutional amendment yesterday, giving 19-year-olds the right to vote—if, in the case of men, they don't have long hair.
        The amendment, which didn't say anything about the length of women's hair, provided that haircuts of youths 19 and 20 must conform to military standards.

---

[12] Bertrand Russell employs this argument in *A History of Western Philosophy*, p. 198.

"When you accept the responsibility of a citizen, you should look like a citizen," said Sen. J. W. Myers of Evanston.[13]

Myers appears to be "reasoning" as follows:

Long-haired young men do not look like citizens. Only persons who look like citizens should be allowed to vote. So no long-haired young men should be given the vote.

This argument is a collector's item. Only rarely does one encounter outside of logic texts an argument which is composed exclusively of absurd statements. (L = long-haired young men, C = persons who look like citizens, V = persons who should be allowed to vote)

31. The preceding argument could be attacked in several ways, including:

It is false that none of our founding fathers looked like citizens. Some of our founding fathers were men who wore their hair long. Hence it is false that no long-haired men look like citizens.

(F = founding fathers, C = persons who look like citizens, L = long-haired men)

32. It is plausible to hold that only contingent statements are empirically verifiable. Arguments 32 and 33 (linked together) attack this view.

Any statement which is entailed by 'It is raining' is empirically

---

[13] "Long Hair Would K.O. Vote Rights," *The Miami News*, February 8, 1969, p. 1-A.

verifiable. Any statement which has the form 'It is raining or . . .' is entailed by 'It is raining.' It follows that all statements of the form 'It is raining or . . .' are empirically verifiable.

(E = statements entailed by 'It is raining,' V = empirically verifiable statements, F = statements having the form 'It is raining or . . .')

33.　　　All statements of the form 'It is raining or . . .' are empirically verifiable. Some tautologies have that form.[14] Hence some tautologous statements are empirically verifiable.

(F, V, T = tautologies)

34.　　　Any policy according to which the university acts as bail bondsman for the student is an *in loco parentis* policy. Students favor all such bail policies. Therefore there is at least one *in loco parentis* policy which is favored by college students.

(B = policies which have the university making bail for its students, L = *in loco parentis* policies, F = policies favored by students)

35.　　　One could miss question two only if one failed to read the assignment. Woodhouse answered question two correctly. So Woodhouse must have read the assignment.

(C = persons who answered question two correctly, R = readers of the assignment, W = persons identical to Woodhouse)

36. Some Renaissance humanists argued:[15]

Syllogisms cannot yield new knowledge. Any fruitful form of thought can give new knowledge. Hence syllogisms are not fruitful forms of thought.

---

[14] For example: It is raining or it is not raining.
[15] See Wilhelm Windelband, *A History of Philosophy*, II, 360.

(S = syllogisms, K = things which can yield new knowledge, F = fruitful forms of thought)

37. Is it possible to obtain knowledge in the empirical sciences? The following syllogism aims to establish a negative answer to this question:

> A statement cannot be known if it could possibly be false. It follows that no statement from the empirical sciences can be known, since any such statement could possibly be false.

(K = statements which can be known, P = statements whose falsity is a possibility, E = statements from the empirical sciences)

38. The preceding argument fails to establish its conclusion because its first premise is false.[16] Argument 38 seeks to demonstrate the falsity of that premise.

> Some statements outside the realm of logic and mathematics can be known. Any statement outside this realm could possibly be false. We conclude that some statements whose falsity is a possibility can be known.

(O = statements outside the realm of logic and mathematics, K = statements which can be known, P = statements whose falsity is a possibility)

39. In defense of the first premise of 37 one could argue:

> A statement cannot be known if it is false. Any false statement is a statement whose falsity is possible. Therefore a statement cannot be known if it could possibly be false.

---

[16] A person who subscribes to this premise is using unreasonably strict standards for *knowledge*.

(K = statements which can be known, F = false statements, P = statements whose falsity is a possibility)

40. Many logicians propose 'implies' as a reading for the "horseshoe" statement connective. This is confused since 'implies' is a relational predicate while the horseshoe symbol is a statement connective. As 40 attempts to prove, statement connectives are not relational predicates.

> Statement connectives can be iterated (repeated); relational predicates cannot.[17] Thus statement connectives are not relational predicates.

(S = statement connectives, I = symbols which can be iterated, R = relational predicates)

41. Scientific explanations are frequently deductive arguments—or can be expressed as such. Consider, for example, this simple explanation of why iron conducts electricity:[18]

> All metals conduct electricity. All iron objects are metallic. So all iron objects are electrical conductors.

(M = metallic objects, C = electrical conductors, I = iron objects)

42. There are synthetic propositions which are nonempty. There

---

[17] For example, S1 makes sense but S2 does not.

    (S1) If Joe comes then if Sam comes Bob comes.
    (S2) Joe killed Sam killed Bob.

For a discussion of this matter see W. V. Quine, *Mathematical Logic*, pp. 23–33 (especially pp. 31–32).

[18] Arthur Pap discusses this explanation in *An Introduction to the Philosophy of Science*, p. 349.

are also a priori propositions which are nonempty. Hence at least one synthetic proposition is a priori.

(S = synthetic propositions, E = empty propositions, P = a priori propositions)

43. In its strictest form the *verifiability criterion of meaning*[19] attributes empirical meaning only to those statements which are in principle conclusively verifiable. Arguments 43 and 44 show that this strict criterion has the embarrassing consequence that some scientific sentences lack empirical meaning.

> Only those statements which are in principle conclusively verifiable are empirically meaningful. Universal statements are not conclusively verifiable even in principle. Therefore such statements lack empirical meaning.

(V = statements which are in principle conclusively verifiable, M = empirically meaningful statements, U = universal statements)

44.   Universal statements lack empirical meaning. Many scientific laws are universal statements. It follows that some laws of science are not empirically meaningful.

(U, M, L = scientific laws)

45.   If you accept the premises of a valid deductive argument, you are logically committed to accepting the conclusion. There are valid deductive arguments which do not beg the question. So not all arguments which beg the question are such that accepting their premises commits one logically to accepting their conclusions.

---

[19]Arguments 151 and 152 also treat the verifiability criterion.

($C =$ arguments such that accepting their premises logically commits one to accepting their conclusions, $V =$ valid deductive arguments, $B =$ question-begging arguments)

46. I attended a zoning hearing at which a builder attempted unsuccessfully to bring about a change in the zoning of a ten-acre block of land. He hoped for a jump from "single-family residences" to "high-density apartments." The builder (a Mr. Emmer) tried to convince the board that his intentions were humanitarian and claimed that he planned to make a profit of *one sixth of one percent* on the project. The objecting neighbors were led by a black minister who told the board, "Any builder who says he plans to make a profit of one sixth of one percent is either a fool or a liar." The minister was advancing a syllogism with a suppressed premise *and* a suppressed conclusion. Supply these statements and assess the argument. ($B =$ builders who say they plan to make a profit of one sixth of one percent, $F =$ persons who are fools or liars, $E =$ persons identical to Emmer)

47. Conclusive proofs are possible in every branch of mathematics. They are also possible in logic. Logic, then, must be a branch of mathematics.

($P =$ disciplines in which conclusive proofs are possible, $M =$ branches of mathematics, $L =$ disciplines identical to logic)

48. A University of Miami student accused of raping a coed (see 109 and 314) was released from jail a month after the second semester began. He petitioned the school for reinstatement of his scholarship while he completed his previous semester's work. The dean of students replied:

Being enrolled as a full-time student is a necessary condition for receiving scholarship aid. Since you aren't currently a full-time student you can't receive aid.

(F = students enrolled full time, S = students receiving scholarship aid, Y = students identical to you)

49. Invalid arguments do not establish their conclusions. There are proofs of the existence of God which are not invalid. This shows that some proofs for God's existence establish their conclusions.

(I = invalid arguments, E = arguments which establish their conclusions, P = proofs of the existence of God)

50. Some contemporary philosophers consider important the question whether there can be a wholly private language, that is, a language which deals only with sensations. The question obviously has implications for philosophy of mind. In *Philosophical Investigations*,[20] Ludwig Wittgenstein held that a private language is impossible. One of his reasons is paraphrased by 50:

> Every language involves rules, and anything which involves rules also involves criteria of correctness (that is, criteria for determining whether the rules are satisfied). Since no private language has criteria of correctness, no languages are private languages.

(L = languages, R = things involving rules, C = things involving criteria of correctness, P = private languages)

51. When the director of campus security was asked (by Rocky Walters) to provide a campus patrolman for a panel discussion of laws on and off the campus, he refused on the grounds that none of his policemen was qualified to speak on campus regulations. He thereby opened himself to the following criticism:

---

[20] See paragraphs 258–259.

No person is qualified to speak on the law unless he knows the law. A person who does not know the law is not qualified to enforce it. None of the campus police is qualified to talk in public about the law. It follows that none of the campus policemen is qualified to enforce the law.

(S = persons qualified to speak on the law, K = persons who know the law, E = persons qualified to enforce the law, P = campus policemen)

52. Human acts are events. There are human acts for which humans are morally responsible. Any act for which a human is morally responsible is free. Free acts are not caused events. So the thesis (of determinism) that all events are caused is false.

(H = human acts, E = events, R = acts for which humans are morally responsible, F = free acts, C = caused events)

53. Logic students often express surprise when they are told that an argument with logically contradictory premises must be valid. Argument 53 shows why this should be so. (It should be noted that even though such arguments are valid, they do not establish their conclusions. See 12.)

Any argument with a logically contradictory premise set has premises which cannot possibly all be true. An argument whose premises cannot possibly all be true is one which cannot possibly have all true premises and a false conclusion. But all arguments which cannot possibly have all true premises and a false conclusion are valid. Therefore all arguments with logically contradictory premises are valid.

(X = arguments having logically contradictory premise sets, Y = arguments whose premises cannot possibly all be true, Z = arguments which cannot possibly have all true premises and a false conclusion, V = valid arguments)

54. In the early fifties a prospector named James Kidd vanished in Arizona, leaving a handwritten will directing that his fortune ($230,000.00) "go into a research or some scientific proof of a soul of the human body which leaves at death." One hundred and thirty individuals and institutions filed for Kidd's estate, including Dr. Richard Spurney, a junior college teacher. Spurney submitted to the court a foot-thick pile of "evidence" which included three unpublished books. He had fifty "proofs" of the existence of the soul. Spurney summarized his main proof as follows:

> Death is decomposition. Hence, what cannot decompose cannot die. But decomposition requires divisibility into parts. Thus what is not divisible into parts cannot die. But divisibility into parts requires matter. Hence what has no matter in it is not divisible into parts and so cannot decompose, and so is necessarily immortal.[21]

This reasoning is paraphrased by 54. It is doubtful that all of the premises in this sorites are true, and Spurney presupposes just what he is supposed to prove (that a human soul exists). Nevertheless it is of interest to determine whether his argument is valid. (After hearing testimony for thirteen weeks, the court awarded the estate to the Barrow Neurological Institute of Phoenix, Arizona.)

Everything which dies decomposes. Anything which decomposes divides into parts. Only material things can be divided

---

[21] "Professor Claims Miner's Jackpot By 'Proving' Soul" (Associated Press), *The Miami Herald*, March 27, 1967, p. 14–A. See also "Neurologists Granted $230,000 Willed For Research Of Soul" (Associated Press), *The Miami News*, October 21, 1967, p. 1–A.

into parts. The human soul is not material. Hence the human soul cannot die.

(X = things which die, Y = things which decompose, Z = divisible things, M = material things, S = human souls)

55. It is possible for a valid argument to appear invalid when examined with the techniques of syllogistic logic. This occurs when validity hinges on features of the argument which are ignored by syllogistic techniques.[22] Consider the following:[23]

Rachel is the mother of Richard. Richard is the father of Robert. The mother of the father is the paternal grandmother. Thus Rachel is the paternal grandmother of Robert.

(A = persons identical to Rachel, B = persons identical to the mother of Richard, C = persons identical to Richard, D = persons identical to the father of Robert, E = mothers of fathers, F = paternal grandmothers, G = persons identical to the paternal grandmother of Robert)

56.   The laws of physics are propositions. These physical laws will hold when all human minds have disappeared. Nothing which will hold when human minds have all disappeared is mind-dependent. So propositions are not mind-dependent.

(L = laws of physics, P = propositions, H = things which will hold when all human minds have disappeared, M = mind-dependent things)

---

[22] For additional examples see 209 and 211.

[23] This argument is discussed by Karl Popper in "Why Are the Calculi of Logic and Arithmetic Applicable to Reality?" *Conjectures and Refutations*, p. 201.

57. The philosopher Berkeley maintained that objects of ordinary experience such as houses, mountains, and rivers do not exist when they are not perceived. He supported this paradoxical contention with the following reasoning.[24]

> Houses, mountains, and rivers are things we perceive. We perceive only ideas.[25] Ideas do not exist unperceived. It follows that houses, mountains, and rivers do not exist unperceived.

(H = houses, mountains, and rivers, P = things we perceive, I = ideas, U = things which exist unperceived)

58. J. S. Mill thought it possible to reason without generalizations, using only particulars. One of his arguments:[26]

> Only language users employ generalizations. No animals have language. But some animals reason. Hence some reasoning beings do not employ generalizations.

(L = language users, G = beings who employ generalizations, A = animals, R = beings who reason)

59. People sometimes regard false sentences as meaningless. In fact a sentence can't be both false and meaningless. One might argue the point as follows:

> Any sentence which says that something not the case is the case, is false. Any sentence which says that something not the

---

[24] *The Principles of Human Knowledge*, pp. 24–25. See 237 and 238 for related Berkeleyan arguments.
[25] The critical premise.
[26] See J. P. Day, "John Stuart Mill," in *A Critical History of Western Philosophy*, p. 344.

case is the case, is a sentence which maintains that something is the case. If a sentence asserts something to be the case, it can't be meaningless. It follows that no sentence is both false and meaningless.

(Y = sentences which say that something not the case is the case, F = false sentences, Z = sentences which say that something is the case, M = meaningless sentences)

60. The preceding sorites dealt with the mistaken belief that *false* sentences are meaningless. Sorites 60 treats the related incorrect belief that *contradictions* are meaningless.

Contradictions are not meaningless. This is a logical consequence of three considerations: (1) every contradictory sentence is logically false, (2) every logically false sentence is false, and (3) false sentences are not meaningless.

(C = contradictions, M = meaningless sentences, L = logically false sentences, F = false sentences)

2 | Valid and Invalid Truth-Functional Arguments

61. If capital punishment deterred capital crimes, then it would be justified. Since it does not deter such crimes, it isn't justified.

(D = Capital punishment deters capital crimes, J = Capital punishment is justified)[27]

62. Philosophers disagree about whether it is correct to say 'I know that I am in pain.' Some who think it correct go on to argue that only I have direct access to my own mental states. One who regards the sentence as incorrect could defend his position with 62.[28]

The sentence 'I know that I am in pain' makes sense only if 'I doubt that I am in pain' does also. The latter sentence does not make sense. Therefore the former doesn't either.

---

[27] In the first section capital letters abbreviate *terms;* in this section (as well as the third) they abbreviate *statements.*

[28] Wittgenstein appears to be using this argument in paragraph 246 of *Philosophical Investigations.*

(K = The sentence 'I know that I am in pain' makes sense, D = The sentence 'I doubt that I am in pain' makes sense)

63. The defendant's statement is incompatible with the plaintiff's testimony. The plaintiff's testimony is false. So the defendant's statement is true.

(D = The defendant's statement is true, P = The plaintiff's testimony is true)

64. Following is one of the major arguments of tobacco spokesmen against the claim that smoking causes lung cancer. Recent research shows the falsity of the first premise.[29]

Lung cancer is more common among male smokers than it is among female smokers. (L)[30] If smoking were the cause of lung cancer, this would not be true. The fact that lung cancer is more common among male smokers means that it is caused by something in the male make-up. It follows that lung cancer is not caused by smoking, but by something in the male make-up.

(L, S = Smoking causes lung cancer, M = Something in the male make-up causes lung cancer)

65. The view that there is no universal moral standard is called *Ethical Relativism*. It can be defended in this way:

Different societies have different moral ideas. (D) If this is so, then there isn't a universal moral standard. Hence there is no such standard. (S)

(D, S)

---

[29] See "Smoking and the Heart," *Newsweek*, July 15, 1968, p. 88.
[30] See convention two in *Student's Preface*.

66.   Argument 65 establishes its conclusion only if its second premise is true. If that premise is true, then there is no difference between the concepts "what people in a society think to be right" and "what *is* right." But there is a difference. (D) So 65 doesn't establish its conclusion. (E)

(E, T = The second premise of 65 is true, D)

67. A radio commercial states, "If you're thinking of orange juice but you're not thinking of *Orange Blossom*, then you're just not thinking of orange juice." The advertisers apparently think this entails the sentence 'If you're thinking of orange juice, then you're thinking of *Orange Blossom*.' Does it? (J = You're thinking of orange juice, B = You're thinking of *Orange Blossom*)

68. A foreign student of my acquaintance who is skeptical about Christianity formulated this argument:

> If (the Christian) God loves all men, then he does not love only one. And if he loves only one man, then he does not love all men. Hence he does not love all men. (A)

(A, O = God loves only one man)

69. Some people regard scientific laws as prescriptive (as rules); others believe that laws *describe*, rather than *prescribe* the behavior of objects. A philosopher in the latter group might defend his view with 69.

> Natural laws are either rules *commanding* physical objects to behave in certain ways or they are statements which *describe* the ways in which they behave. If they are the former, then the notion of a physical object "disobeying" a natural law would make sense. But this notion does not make sense. (N) Conse-

quently, natural laws are statements which describe how physical objects behave. (D)

(C = Natural laws are rules commanding physical objects to behave in certain ways, D, N)

70.   If the statement 'There is no truth' is true, then it's not true. Thus it isn't true. (T)

(T)

71.   We can't win the war on poverty without spending money. So if we do spend money we will conquer poverty.

(W = We win the war on poverty, S = We spend money)

72.   If the earth revolved around the sun but didn't rotate on its axis, there would be no day and night. Since there is day and night, either the earth does not revolve or it both revolves and rotates.

(S = The earth revolves around the sun, A = The earth rotates on its axis, D = There is day and night)

73.   The earth does not revolve or it both revolves and rotates. If its rotation is a necessary condition for its revolution, then any evidence of its revolution is also evidence for its rotation. Hence any evidence that the earth revolves is also evidence that it rotates.

(See 72; S, A, E = Any evidence that the earth revolves is evidence that it rotates)

74. Is the following statement (call it 'S') logically contradictory?

If it is raining then it isn't raining.

As a step toward answering this question determine whether S entails 'It is raining and it isn't raining.' ($R =$ It is raining)

75.   S isn't contradictory unless it entails all contradictions. S does not entail every contradiction unless it entails 'It is raining and it isn't raining.' Since S does not entail this sentence it is not contradictory.

($C = $ S is contradictory, $A = $ S entails every contradiction, $B = $ S entails 'It is raining and it isn't raining')

76.   S (see 74) is logically equivalent to 'It isn't raining.' (A) This is a consequence of the following facts: S is logically equivalent to 'Either it isn't raining or it isn't raining.' (B) The latter sentence is logically equivalent to 'It isn't raining.' (C) If both of these equivalences hold, then S must be logically equivalent to 'It isn't raining.'

(A, B, C)

77. Does 'It is raining *if and only if* it isn't raining' entail 'It is raining and it isn't raining'? ($R =$ It is raining)

78. The absent-minded coffee drinker reasons:

Since my spoon is dry I must not have sugared my coffee, because the spoon would be wet if I had stirred the coffee and I wouldn't have stirred it unless I had put sugar in it.

($D = $ My spoon is dry, $X = $ I sugared my coffee, $Y = $ I stirred my coffee)

79. Some philosophers say 'You know *only indirectly* that I have pain.' They use this alleged fact to support a particular view about the nature of mind (mind-body dualism). In "The Privacy of Experience," [31] Norman Malcolm argues that there is something wrong with the sentence mentioned above. His reasoning is summarized in 79.

> In the sentence 'I know I have pain,' the words 'I know' serve no purpose. If this is so, then there is something wrong with saying that I know "directly" that I have pain. But it would be correct to say that you know only "indirectly" that I have pain only in case it would be correct to say that I know directly that I have pain. Hence there is something wrong with saying that you know only indirectly that I have pain.

(P = The words 'I know' serve some purpose in the sentence 'I know I have pain,' D = It is correct to say that I know directly that I have pain, I = It is correct to say that you know only indirectly that I have pain)

80.   If both premises of 30 are true, then there is such a thing as the "look of a citizen." But there is no such thing. Therefore neither premise is true.

(F = The first premise of 30 is true, S = The second premise of 30 is true, L = There is such a thing as the "look of a citizen")

81. Medieval scholars denied the possibility of a complete vacuum. One of their reasons is founded on a medieval belief about motion.[32]

> The speed of an object varies in inverse proportion to the resistance provided by the medium in which the object is moving. (S) Assuming this is so, then if there exists a perfect vacuum

---

[31] In *Epistemology: New Essays in the Theory of Knowledge*, ed. by Avrum Stroll, p. 151.
[32] See Herbert Butterfield, *The Origins of Modern Science*, p. 16.

any body moving through it would have infinite speed. However, no body could move with infinite speed—even in a vacuum. So there is no perfect vacuum. (V)

(S, V, I = Any body moving through a perfect vacuum would have infinite speed)

82. Change the first premise of 80 to 'If *either* premise of 30 is true, then there is such a thing as the "look of a citizen."' Evaluate the resulting argument. (See 80.)

83. It is common today for theologians to maintain that the Genesis creation story should not be viewed as literal description. But it is surprising to find that the third-century church father Origen shared this position.[33] One of his arguments is paraphrased by 83.

If the creation story is a true literal description, then for the first three days of the earth's existence there was no sun. The concept of "day" is defined by reference to the sun. (D) It cannot both be the case that the concept is so defined and that the earth existed three days before the sun was created. From this it follows that the creation story in Genesis is not true literal description. (L)

(L, F = For the first three days of the earth's existence there was no sun, D)

84. Ordinarily a conditional is logically weaker than the conjunction of its antecedent and consequent. Does a conditional ever entail such a conjunction? Does 'If two is even or not even, *then* two is a prime' entail 'Two is even or not even, *and* two is a prime'? (E = Two is even, P = Two is a prime)

---

[33] See Hick, *Philosophy of Religion*, p. 9.

85. A. J. Ayer seems to advance the following argument in *Language, Truth and Logic*:[34]

> If either subjectivism or utilitarianism is correct, then ethical concepts are reducible to empirical concepts. However, neither of these ethical positions is correct. It follows that ethical concepts cannot be reduced to empirical concepts. (R)

(S = Subjectivism is correct, U = Utilitarianism is correct, R)

86.   Joe is fat. (J) So either Sally is ugly or she is not ugly.

(J, S = Sally is ugly)

87. The preceding argument is a peculiar and apparently worthless argument. Why, then, should it have tested out as it did? Argument 87 offers an explanation.

> Argument 86 is valid if and only if it is logically impossible for its premise to be true while its conclusion is false. It is logically impossible for its conclusion to be false; and if this is so, then it is logically impossible for its premise to be true while its conclusion is false. Thus 86 is valid. (V)

(V, A = It is logically impossible for the premise of 86 to be true while its conclusion is false, B = It is logically impossible for the conclusion of 86 to be false)

88.   If intelligence is wholly hereditary and provided that identical twins have the same heredity, then being raised in separate households will not reduce the similarity of intelligence between two identical twins. But it does reduce the similarity. (R) Identical

---

[34] See pp. 104–5.

twins come from a common sperm and egg. (C) This means that
they have identical heredity. Therefore intelligence is not entirely hereditary. (H)[35]

$(H, I =$ Identical twins have identical heredity, R, C)

89.   If some term in a theory is defined by means of a second
term which has been previously defined with the help of the first,
then there is a circular chain of definitions. If no term in the
theory is defined by means of a second term which has been
defined previously with the aid of the first term, then *all* the
terms in the theory are defined only if there is an infinite regress
of definitions. Hence a necessary condition for defining *all* the
terms in a theory is having either an infinite regress of definitions
or a circular definitional chain.[36]

$(S =$ Some term in a theory is defined by means of a second term
which has been previously defined with the help of the first term,
$C =$ There is a circular chain of definitions, $A =$ All the terms in a
theory are defined, $R =$ There is an infinite regress of definitions)

90. A Volkswagen ad features a photo of a street of identical houses.
In front of every home (twenty-three in all) is parked a red-and-
white Volkswagen station wagon. Under the photo is this message:

> If the world looked like this, and you wanted to buy a
> car that sticks out a little, you probably wouldn't buy a
> Volkswagen Station Wagon. But in case you haven't
> noticed, the world doesn't look like this. So if you've
> wanted to buy a car that sticks out a little, you know
> just what to do.

---

[35] See H. H. Newman, F. N. Freeman, and K. J. Holzinger, *Twins: A
Study of Heredity and Environment.*
[36] See Carl Hempel, *Philosophy of Natural Science,* pp. 87–88.

Assume that 'you know just what to do' means (in this context) you will buy a Volkswagen Station Wagon. Is the argument valid? (If it is invalid does that make the ad defective?) (W = The world looks like this, S = You want a car that sticks out a little, V = You will buy a Volkswagen Station Wagon)

91. In the second chapter of II Kings Elijah asks Elisha for a "double share" of his spirit. Elisha replies:

> You have asked a hard thing; yet, if you see me as I am
> being taken from you, it shall be so for you; but if you
> do not see me, it shall not be so.

Does Elisha's statement entail 'You will receive a double share of my spirit if and only if you see me as I am being taken from you'? (A = You have asked a hard thing, S = You see me as I am being taken from you, R = You receive a double share of my spirit)

92.   If arithmetic could be reduced to truth-functional logic, then the existence of a mechanical decision procedure for the latter would be a sufficient condition for the existence of such a procedure for the former. There is a mechanical decision procedure for truth-functional logic, but none for arithmetic. Consequently arithmetic is not reducible to truth-functional logic. (R)

(R, T = There is a mechanical decision procedure for truth-functional logic, A = There is a mechanical decision procedure for arithmetic)

93. Some philosophers (called "identity theorists") maintain that consciousness is a process in the brain. Argument 93 is a common criticism of this view.

Consciousness can't be a process in the brain without the

sentence 'Jones feels a pain but nothing is happening inside his skull' being a logical contradiction. Now, that sentence isn't a contradiction. Therefore consciousness isn't a process in the brain. (C)

(C, L = The sentence 'Jones feels a pain but nothing is happening inside his skull' is a logical contradiction)

94. The identity theorist U. T. Place believes the preceding argument to be mistaken. His criticism of it is paraphrased by 94.[37]

The first premise of 93 is true only on the condition that the sentence 'Consciousness is a process in the brain' is a definition. However, that sentence is a scientific hypothesis, not a definition. The falsity of the first premise of 93 is sufficient to show the argument defective. Hence 93 is defective. (B)

(T = The first premise of 93 is true, A = The sentence 'Consciousness is a process in the brain' is a definition, H = The sentence 'Consciousness . . . brain' is a scientific hypothesis, B)

95.   Unless 93 is invalid or has one or more false premises, the identity theory is wrong. While 93 is valid, it does have at least one false premise. It follows that the identity theory is correct. (C)

(V = 93 is valid, F = 93 has at least one false premise, C)

96. Norman Malcolm[38] attacks the identity theory in the following way (among others):

---

[37] See Place, "Is Consciousness a Brain Process?" *British Journal of Psychology,* XLVII (1956), 44–50.
[38] See "[Abstract of] Scientific Materialism and the Identity Theory," *The Journal of Philosophy,* LX (Oct. 24, 1963), 662–63.

If brain phenomena are identical with mental phenomena, then mental phenomena will have spatial location if and only if brain phenomena do. Brain phenomena can be located spatially. (B) If mental phenomena are spatially locatable then it will be meaningful to assign spatial location to a thought. It is not meaningful to do this. (A) So brain phenomena and mental phenomena are not identical. (I)

(I, M = Mental phenomena have spatial location, B, A)

97. I turn on the Giants–Browns game in the middle of the second half and see Pete Gogolak kicking off. I reason:

The Giants must have just scored. (S) Because Gogolak does not kick off except at the start of a half and after a Giants' score. Gogolak just kicked off, but this is not the beginning of a half.

(S, K = Gogolak has just kicked off, B = It is the beginning of a half)

98. Stopped at a traffic light I notice that water is leaking onto the road from the car beside mine. I make the following inference:

Either their radiator is boiling over or their air conditioner is on. Their windows are up even though the temperature is 90 degrees. If this is so[39] they must be air conditioning. Thus their radiator isn't boiling over. (B)

(B, A = They are air conditioning, W = Their windows are up, T = The temperature is 90 degrees)

---

[39] See convention three in *Student's Preface*.

99. In the sixth Meditation,[40] Descartes argues:

> Body is by nature divisible. (B) If so and if mind and body are one and the same, then mind is also divisible. However, the mind is entirely indivisible. (M) It follows that the mind and body are not the same. (S)

(B, S, M)

100. When I pick up the pizza should I leave the kids in the car?

> I can't take them both out. If I take Mike but not Amy, Amy will cry. I won't let that happen. So I will not take either of them.

$(M =$ I take Mike out of the car, $A =$ I take Amy out of the car, $C =$ Amy cries)

101. How ought sentences of the form 'Only A are B' be put into standard form? For example, should S1 be translated as S2 or S3?

(S1) Only intelligent persons are physicists.
(S2) All intelligent persons are physicists.
(S3) All physicists are intelligent persons.

Argument 101 attempts to answer this question.

> S1 translates into standard form either as S2 or as S3 (but not both). If the former, then the truth of S1 is both a necessary and a sufficient condition for the truth of S2. S1 is true, but S2 is false. Therefore S1 translates into standard form as S3. (B)

---

[40] *Meditations on First Philosophy*, p. 81.

($A = S1$ translates into standard form as S2, B, $C = S1$ is true, $D = S2$ is true)

102.   If there are an infinite number of points in a finite line L, then if those points have size, L will be infinitely long, and if they do not have size, L will have no length. But line L is neither infinitely long nor without length. This proves that there are not an infinite number of points in L. (I)[41]

(I, S = The points in line L have size, A = L is infinitely long, L = L has length)

103. Pascal's famous wager[42] is paraphrased by 103.

If I believe in God, then (1) if he exists I gain, and (2) if he doesn't then (at least) I don't lose. If, on the other hand, I don't believe, then (1) if God exists I lose, and (2) if he doesn't I don't gain. From this it follows that if I believe I'll either gain or (at least) not lose, while if I don't believe I'll either lose or (at best) fail to gain.

See 26 for an observation about anyone who would use this argument as grounds for belief in God. (B = I believe in God, E = God exists, G = I gain, L = I lose)

104. (DIFFICULT)

If any one of the three positions of hard determinism, soft determinism, and indeterminism[43] is correct, then the other two are

---

[41] This argument is discussed by Peter Caws in *The Philosophy of Science*, p. 147. Caws attributes it to Zeno.
[42] See his *Pensées*, number 233.
[43] For an explanation of these three terms see William James's essay "The

mistaken. So one of these three positions is correct, and the other two are incorrect.

(H = Hard determinism is correct, S = Soft determinism is correct, I = Indeterminism is correct)

105. (DIFFICULT) The following puzzle appears in *101 Puzzles in Thought and Logic*, by C. R. Wylie, Jr.:[44]

> The personnel director of a firm in speaking of three men the company was thinking of hiring once said,
>
> > "We need Brown and if we need Jones then we need Smith, if and only if we need either Brown or Jones and don't need Smith."
>
> If the company actually needed more than one of the men, which ones were they?

(Read no further if you want to solve the puzzle on your own.) Let the first premise of 105 be the personnel director's statement. The second premise is 'We need more than one of the men.' The conclusion is the answer to the puzzle: 'We need Jones and Smith, but do not need Brown.' By proving 105 to be valid you prove that this is the correct answer to the puzzle (but of course you don't show the reasoning by which the solution was discovered). (B = We need Brown, J = We need Jones, S = We need Smith)

Dilemma of Determinism" in *Essays in Pragmatism*, ed. by Alburey Castell. See especially pp. 40–41.
[44] Dover Publications, Inc., New York, 1957, puzzle 42. Reprinted through permission of the publisher.

3 | Valid Truth-Functional Arguments

106. The gang is playing Rummy. After the first hand is dealt Howard asks, "Are aces high or low?" David reasons:

> Either Howard has an ace or he is very crafty. But he isn't crafty at all. (C)[45] Therefore Howard has an ace. (A)

(A, C)

107. The simplest version of the teleological argument for the existence of God:

> There is design in the world. (A) Design implies a designer. Thus there must be a designer of the world. (B)

(A, B)

108.　　　Does the word 'pencil' refer to the class of pencils? The answer is 'No.' A proof of this follows: If the word referred to the class of pencils, then we could make the claim that the class of

---

[45] See conventions one and two in *Student's Preface.*

pencils is very large by uttering the sentence 'Pencil is very large.' But we cannot make the claim by uttering this sentence. (C)[46]

(R = The word 'pencil' refers to the class of pencils, C)

109. A University of Miami coed charged a fellow student with rape. Campus opinion was split regarding the girl's veracity. Some persons who supported the girl gave the following as a reason:

> The girl knew (because of the special circumstances of the incident) that publicity about the matter would wreck her life. (P) If so, then she wouldn't have telephoned the police unless she had actually been raped. Since she did call the police, she must have been raped.

Persons sympathetic to the boy advanced 314 on his behalf. The Dade County Grand Jury refused to indict the boy. (P, T = She telephoned the police, R = She was raped)

110. A frequently aired criticism of the proposal for an all-volunteer army is that such an army would be more likely to attempt a coup d'etat. Argument 110 attacks this criticism.

> All the high-ranking officers in our present army are volunteers. (V) Military coups are engineered by high-ranking officers. (E) Provided that both of the preceding statements are true, an all-volunteer army would not increase the chances of a military

---

[46] This argument is advanced by William Alston in *Philosophy of Language,* p. 15.

take-over. Consequently the probability of a military coup would not be increased by the institution of an all-volunteer army. (*I*)

(V, E, I)

111. Prove that these four sentences constitute an inconsistent set by deriving some contradiction from them.

> Every event is caused. (E)
>
> If this is so, then there aren't any situations in which a person could act in a way different from the way in which he did act.
>
> People are morally responsible for (at least some of) their actions. (R)
>
> A necessary condition for people being morally responsible for their actions is the existence of situations in which a person could act in a way different from the one in which he acted.

(E, $S =$ There are situations in which a person could act in a way other than the one in which he acted, R)

112. This argument provides an explanation for the rapidly rising costs of college education:

> Labor costs are rising in all sectors of the economy. (*L*) In most areas these costs are offset by increased worker productivity (as a result of automation). (*O*) Increased labor costs in the field of higher education (faculty raises) are not offset by increased productivity (number of students taught). (*E*) If all of the preceding is true, then the cost of college education is increasing at a rate which is well above the general cost of living. We can

conclude that the cost of higher education is increasing at a rate well above the general cost of living. (C)

(L, O, E, C)

113. Some thinkers[47] have maintained that all sentences which deny existence are false. Argument 113 [48] indicates how one might arrive at this strange view.

> The sentence 'Santa Claus does not exist' (call it 'S') is about Santa Claus. (A) If S is about Santa Claus, then there is such a thing as Santa Claus. But if there is such a thing as Santa Claus, then S is false. It follows that S is false. (F)

$(A, E = \text{There is such a thing as Santa Claus}, F)$

114. Sometimes an explanation for a person's decision can be set out in the form of an argument, where the argument's conclusion states the decision made. Argument 114, for example, explains my decision to drive to school this morning on Old Cutler Road rather than on Dixie Highway.

> It's raining. (R) If so, then it will be safer to take the road on which I will have to make fewer quick stops. Old Cutler will

---

[47] In 1903 Bertrand Russell wrote:

> Being belongs to whatever can be counted. If A be any term that can be counted as one, it is plain that A is something, and therefore that A is. 'A is not' must always be either false or meaningless.

The Principles of Mathematics, para. 427. By 1905 he had rejected this position.

[48] This argument is discussed by Richard Cartwright in "Negative Existentials," *The Journal of Philosophy,* LVII (1960), 629–30. Cartwright believes the second premise to be false.

involve fewer quick stops. (*F*) If it will be safer to take the road which involves fewer quick stops and if Old Cutler is that road, then I will take Old Cutler. So I will take Old Cutler Road. (*O*)

Obviously the actual thinking which led to this decision was not as formalized as this argument. Perhaps I thought, "I'd better take Old Cutler because of all the stops on Dixie." Nevertheless 114 makes explicit the logic involved in the reasoning. (R, S = It will be safer to take the road which will involve fewer quick stops, F, O)

115.   If there were a natural connection between words and the ideas they stand for, then all men would share a common language. However, there are many languages. If the connection between words and the ideas they represent is not natural, then it is the result of arbitrary choice. This proves that the connection between words and the ideas for which they stand is the consequence of arbitrary choice. (*A*)[49]

(N = There is a natural connection between words and the ideas they stand for, C = All men share a common language, A)

116.   We can't both conduct a war and solve our domestic problems. Therefore avoiding war is a necessary condition for the solution of our domestic problems.

(W = We engage in war, D = We solve our domestic problems)

117.   If Cain married his sister, their marriage was incestuous. If he didn't marry his sister, then Adam and Eve were not the progenitors of the entire human race. It follows that Adam and Eve were the progenitors of the whole human race only if Cain's marriage was incestuous.

---

[49] John Locke employs this argument in *An Essay Concerning Human Understanding*, II, 8.

(S = Cain married his sister, I = Cain's marriage was incestuous, P = Adam and Eve were the progenitors of the entire human race)

118. I utter the sentence 'Do you want Mike and I to get submarines?' and then begin to wonder whether it is grammatically correct. I convince myself that it isn't in the following way.

> The sentence is correct if and only if the sentence 'Do you want I to get submarines?' is correct. Obviously the latter is bad grammar. So the former is also ungrammatical.

(X = The sentence 'Do you want Mike and I to get submarines?' is grammatically correct, Y = The sentence 'Do you want I to get submarines?' is grammatically correct)

119. One version of the "pragmatic" justification of induction:[50]

> If there are uniformities in nature, then induction will work. If there is a method of inference about the future which works, then there are uniformities in nature. Conclusion: if induction does not work, then no method of inference about the future will work.

(U = There are uniformities in nature, I = Induction works, M = There is a method of inference about the future which works)

120. Excedrin Headache Number 83; the university president:

> Either we do classified research for the federal government or we don't do it. Doing it means inviting student-faculty protest. Not doing it means being short of funds. We will have to cut

---

[50] Wesley C. Salmon discusses this argument in *The Foundations of Scientific Inference*, pp. 52–54.

back our academic program if we are short of funds. So either we invite protest by the students and faculty or we curtail our academic program.

(R = We do classified federal research, P = We invite student-faculty protest, F = We are short of funds, C = We curtail our academic program)

121. The philosopher William Alston draws a conclusion about language from an examination of arguments 252 and 253.[51] He reasons:

> One of the arguments in the set 252, 253 is valid, and one of them is invalid. If this is so, then the sentence 'Joe Carpenter sells insurance in our town' is of a different logical form from the sentence 'Someone sells insurance in our town.' These two sentences are of a different logical form only if there is a fundamental difference between a proper name (like 'Joe Carpenter') and a locution like 'someone.' Hence a fundamental difference exists between proper names and terms like 'someone.' (D)

(A = One of the arguments in the set 252, 253 is valid, B = One of the arguments in the set 252, 253 is invalid, C = The sentence 'Joe Carpenter sells insurance in our town' is of a different logical form from the sentence 'Someone sells insurance in our town,' D)

122. The first premise of the preceding argument was symbolized as 'A and B.' Could it have been symbolized as 'A and not-A'? Argument 122 shows that the latter symbolization would be mistaken.

> If the first sentence in 121 can be correctly symbolized as 'A and not-A,' then provided that 'A and not-A' is logically false,

---

[51] See Alston, *Philosophy of Language*, pp. 3–4.

the first sentence in 121 is also logically false. While 'A and not-A' is logically false, the first sentence of 121 is not. It must follow, therefore, that the first sentence in the argument cannot be symbolized correctly as 'A and not-A.' (C)

(C, A = 'A and not-A' is logically false, B = The first sentence in 121 is logically false)

123. Consider this argument:

> (A1) Scherer is a florist.
>   Therefore Scherer exists.

Is A1 valid? Argument 123 purports to prove it valid and 124 attempts to prove it invalid. (Since 123 and 124 are both valid and their conclusions are contradictory, at least one must contain a false premise.)

It is logically impossible for Scherer to be a florist without existing. (A) If this is so, then it is logically impossible for the premise of A1 to be true and the conclusion false. A1 is valid if and only if it is logically impossible for its premise to be true while its conclusion is false. Thus A1 is valid. (V)

(A, B = It is logically impossible for the premise of A1 to be true and the conclusion false, V)

124. Argument 124 compares A1 of the preceding exercise with the following two arguments:

> (A2) Scherer is not a florist.
>   Therefore Scherer exists.
>
> (A3) Scherer does not exist.
>   Therefore Scherer is a florist.

Argument 124:

>   A1 is valid if and only if A2 is. A2 is valid if and only if
>   A3 is.[52] A3 is not valid. (D) So A1 isn't either. (B)

$(B, C = $ A2 is valid, $D)$

125.   I am not going to be drafted. (D) The reason: (I am so far
down the manpower priority list that) I won't be drafted unless
there is a nuclear war. But if there is such a war they won't draft
me either (since there will not be adequate time for the process).

$(D, N = $ There is a nuclear war$)$

126. Argument 126 indicates how Boyle's Law may be derived from
the kinetic theory of gases.[53]

>   The pressure exerted by a gas in a container results from the
>   impacts of the molecules upon the containing walls and is
>   quantitatively equal to the average value of the total momentum
>   that the molecules deliver per second to a unit square of the
>   wall area. (A) If this is so, then the pressure of a gas is inversely
>   proportional to its volume and is directly proportional to the mean
>   kinetic energy of its molecules. The mean kinetic energy of the
>   molecules of a fixed mass of gas remains constant as long as the
>   temperature remains constant. (C) If the pressure of a gas is
>   inversely proportional to its volume and directly proportional to
>   the mean kinetic energy of its molecules, and if the mean kinetic
>   energy of the molecules of a fixed mass of gas remains constant
>   as long as the temperature is held constant, then the pressure

---

[52] This premise is based on the logical principle that if one statement
entails a second, the denial of the second entails the denial of the first.
[53] See Hempel, *Philosophy of Natural Science*, p. 73.

of a fixed mass of gas at a constant temperature will be inversely proportional to its volume. It follows from the above that the pressure of a fixed mass of gas at constant temperature is inversely proportional to the volume of the gas. *(D)*

$(A, B = $ The pressure of a gas is inversely proportional to its volume and is directly proportional to the mean kinetic energy of its molecules, $C, D)$

127.   If minds are wholly private, then I cannot know about any individual other than myself that he has a mind. Having a mind is a necessary condition for being a person. *(N)* If this is true,[54] then if I cannot know that any individual besides myself has a mind, then I also cannot know that any other individual is a person. So if I can know about even one individual other than myself that he is a person, then it is false that minds are completely private.

$(W = $ Minds are wholly private, $M = $ I can know that some individual other than myself has a mind, $N, P = $ I can know that some individual other than myself is a person$)$

128.   Ninety-six percent of those persons who have a manic-depressive identical twin are themselves manic-depressive, while only 23% of those persons who have a manic-depressive sibling are themselves manic-depressive. If this is true, then assuming that identical twins have identical heredity and that most siblings do not, heredity must be an important factor in the cause of manic-depression. While most siblings do not have identical heredity, identical twins do. Hence hereditary factors are important in the causation of manic-depression. *(H)*[55]

---

[54] See convention three in *Student's Preface.*
[55] See Franz J. Kallmann, *Heredity in Health and Mental Disorder,* p. 124.

(A = 96% of those persons who have a manic-depressive identical twin are themselves manic-depressive, B = Only 23% of those persons who have a manic-depressive sibling are themselves manic-depressive, C = Identical twins have identical heredity, D = Most siblings do not have identical heredity, H)

129. Consider these sentences:

(S)   The universe was created five minutes ago.
(Not-S) The universe was not created five minutes ago.

Some people would maintain that S is meaningless (since it is neither verifiable nor falsifiable) and that Not-S is true. This will involve a person in a contradiction if he accepts two additional very plausible statements. Demonstrate this by showing that the following four statements entail some obvious contradiction.

S is meaningless.
Not-S is true.
S is meaningful if and only if Not-S is meaningful.
Not-S is true only if it is meaningful.

(A = S is meaningful, T = Not-S is true, B = Not-S is meaningful)

130. I cut the strange news item quoted in exercise 30 from the newspaper and posted it on my office door. Later, when I decided to include it in this exercise book, I had to track down the date of the newspaper from which I had clipped it, as well as the number of the page on which it had appeared. The following reasoning simplified the task:

The clipping is from the *Miami News*. (A) Part of a Herblock cartoon is on the back of the clipping. (B) The *News* carries

Herblock cartoons only on Saturdays. (C) All of these facts taken together imply that the clipping was cut from a Saturday edition of the News. The subject of the cartoon is the navy's investigation of the Pueblo incident. (E) If part of a Herblock cartoon is on the back and that cartoon deals with the Pueblo investigation, then the clipping was taken from a paper printed in the late winter of 1969. The News always prints Herblock cartoons at the bottom of page 2-A. (G) If so, then if the clipping is from the News and has a Herblock cartoon on the back the clipping must have appeared at the bottom of page 1-A of the News. It follows from the above that the clipping was cut from the bottom of page 1-A of a Saturday edition of the News published in the late winter of 1969.

(A, B, C, D = The clipping is from a Saturday edition of the *News*, E, F = The clipping is from a paper printed in the late winter of 1969, G, H = The clipping is from the bottom of page 1-A of the *News*)

131. Many passages in Plato's dialogues are devoted to showing defects in definitions of general terms. In the dialogue *Euthyphro*,[56] for example, Plato (in the person of Socrates) attacks this definition of 'piety': *Piety* means what is pleasing to the gods. His criticism is paraphrased by 131 and 132. (Some of the premises in these arguments seem absurd to us, but they would not have appeared so to Plato's contemporaries.)

The gods quarrel. (Q) If they quarrel at all, then they quarrel over what is just and good. Anyone is pleased by what he thinks just and good, and displeased by what he thinks unjust and bad. If this is so, and if the gods quarrel over what is just and good, then one thing can please one god while displeasing another.

---

[56] *The Dialogues of Plato*, trans. by B. Jowett, I, 388–91.

Therefore one thing can please one god and displease another.
(O)

(*Q, J* = The gods quarrel over what is just and good, *P* = Anyone
is pleased by what he thinks just and good, *D* = Anyone is displeased
by what he thinks unjust and bad, *O*)

132.   One thing can please one god and displease another. (O)
If this is so and if *piety* means what is pleasing to the gods, then
one thing can be both pious and impious. But this is impossible.
So *piety* does not mean what is pleasing to the gods. (M)

(*O, M, B* = One thing can be both pious and impious)

133. Consider these two sentences:

(S1) Joe knows that it is both raining and not raining.
(S2) Joe knows that it is either raining or not raining.

Are these sentences necessarily true, necessarily false, or empirical?
One plausible answer is "They are both empirical"; another is "S1
is necessarily false and S2 is necessarily true." These answers, though
plausible, are mistaken. The correct answer (plus proof that it is
correct) is given in 133 and 134.

         One cannot know what is false. If so, then it is logically im-
possible to know what is necessarily false. If this is logically
impossible, then the necessary falsity of 'It is both raining and
not raining' is a sufficient condition for the necessary falsity of
S1. The sentence 'It is both raining and not raining' is necessarily
false. (A) Consequently S1 is also necessarily false. (B)

(*K* = One can know what is false, *I* = It is logically impossible to
know what is necessarily false, *A, B*)

134.   It is logically possible that S2 is true. (X) It is logically possible that Joe believes it to be false that it is either raining or not raining. (Y) If this is so then the falsity of S2 is a logical possibility. If it is logically possible that S2 is true and also logically possible that it is false, then S2 is empirical. Thus S2 is empirical. (E)

$(X, Y, Z =$ It is logically possible that S2 is false, $E)$

135. S1 is the thesis of *indeterminism;* S2 the thesis of *determinism:*

(S1) There is an event which is caused by no event.

(S2) Every event is caused by some event.

Argument 135 provides a (weak) defense of S2.

S1 can be proved true only if every event can be examined. We cannot examine all events. (E) S1 is the denial of S2. (D) If S1 is S2's denial, then the former can be proved true if and only if the latter can be proved false. Hence S2 cannot be proved false. (F)

$(T =$ S1 can be proved true, $E, D, F)$

136. An ancient Chinese dilemma:[57]

If the world is disordered, it cannot be reformed unless a sage appears. But no sage can appear if the world is disordered. It follows that the world cannot be reformed if it is disordered.

$(D =$ The world is disordered, $R =$ The world can be reformed, $S =$ A sage appears)

---

[57] See Arthur Waley, *Three Ways of Thought in Ancient China,* p. 10, n. 1.

137. The score stands at Miami 16—Penn State 21, as a result of a Hurricane touchdown. Now Coach Tate must decide whether to send in a one-point or a two-point play. His reasoning (which, of course, takes place in a flash) may be represented as follows:

> Seventeen points plus a touchdown will put us ahead, but so will 16 points plus a touchdown. On the other hand, 17 points plus a field goal will not even give us a tie. (C) If all of this is so, then there is no advantage in scoring just one point. Eighteen points plus a field goal will give us a tie. (E) If this is true, then there is something to be gained by attempting the two-point conversion. Therefore there is no advantage in scoring one point, but there is something to be gained by trying a two-point play.

($A = 17$ points plus a touchdown will put us ahead, $B = 16$ points plus touchdown will put us ahead, C, $D =$ There is an advantage in scoring one point, E, $F =$ There is something to be gained by attempting the two-point play)

138. If the score (in the game mentioned in the previous exercise) had been Miami 13—Penn State 21, Tate might have reasoned:

> We will win the game only if we score another touchdown, make a two-point conversion and a one-point conversion. If it is true that we won't win the game without making those three scores, then we won't win the game unless we make a conversion now. If making a conversion now is a necessary condition for winning, then failing to make a conversion now will result in a loss of momentum. If we can prevent a loss of momentum only if we make a conversion now, then we should attempt the easier conversion now. If we should attempt the easier conversion now, then we should attempt the one-point play now. So we should attempt the one-point play now. (O)

(W = We win the game, S = We score another touchdown, make a two-point conversion and a one-point conversion, N = We make a conversion now, L = The team loses momentum, E = We should attempt the easier conversion now, O)

139.   If there is justice in this life, then there is no need for a future life. If, on the other hand, there isn't justice in our earthly existence, then we have no reason to think that God is just. But if we don't have reason to believe God to be just, then there is no reason to think that he will provide a future life for us. Therefore either there is no need for a future life or there is no reason to believe that God will provide such a life.[58]

(J = There is justice in this life, N = There is need for a future life, A = We have reason to think that God is just, P = There is reason to believe that God will provide us with a future life)

140. In William Harvey's day it was generally accepted that blood is created in the heart and flows from that organ only in an outward direction. Harvey's main attack on this theory is summarized by 140.[59]

In an hour, a man's heart throws out more blood than his own weight. (H) If this is so and if blood flows only outward from the heart, then the heart creates more blood in an hour than the weight of a man. But this is impossible. If a man's heart throws out more blood than his weight in an hour's time, the blood must circulate through the body and reenter the heart. It follows that the received doctrine (blood flowing only out of the heart) is false, and that the new doctrine (circulation and reentry) is true.

---

[58] This reasoning is advanced by David Hume in *An Inquiry Concerning Human Understanding*, pp. 150–51.
[59] See Butterfield, *The Origins of Modern Science*, pp. 64–65.

(H, O = Blood flows only outward from the heart, A = The heart creates more blood in an hour than the weight of a man, C = The blood circulates through the body and reenters the heart)

141. A humanities test contains the following multiple-choice question:

> Plato was:
>
> (a) the teacher of Socrates;
> (b) the teacher of Aristotle;
> (c) the teacher of Plotinus;
> (d) all of the above;
> (e) none of the above.

A thinking student who knows that Plato taught Aristotle but did not teach Socrates can be sure of answering the question correctly even if he has never heard of Plotinus. He reasons:

> Plato taught Aristotle. If this is so, then the correct answer is either (b) or (d). (d) is the correct answer only if Plato taught Socrates. Since Plato was not Socrates' teacher, the correct answer has to be (b).

(A = Plato taught Aristotle, B = The correct answer is (b), D = The correct answer is (d), S = Plato taught Socrates)

142. In *Foundations of the Metaphysics of Morals*,[60] Kant argues:

> If moral theory is studied empirically, then examples of conduct will be considered. And if examples of conduct are considered, principles for selecting examples will be employed.

---

[60] P. 25. Compare this argument with 23.

But if such principles are being used, then moral theory is not being studied empirically. Conclusion: moral theory is not studied empirically. (M)

(M, E = Examples of conduct are considered, P = Principles for selecting examples are employed)

143. St. Thomas Aquinas may be viewed as employing the following reasoning in his third cosmological argument.[61]

> Every contingent being came into existence at some time. (C) Time stretches infinitely into the past. (I) If time does go back infinitely into the past, then if every contingent being came into existence at some time there must have been a time before any contingent being existed. If there was such a time, then if there are contingent beings at present either some contingent beings have created themselves or there is a necessary being which has created some contingent beings. There are contingent beings today. (B) No contingent being created itself. Therefore there must be a necessary being which has created some contingent beings. (N)

(C, I, A = There was a time before any contingent being existed, B, D = Some contingent beings have created themselves, N)

144. A father wondering whether his baby son is awake (and hoping that he is, so that they can play) could use the following reasoning to excuse his opening the door to the baby's room.

> Mike's rubber horse squeaked. (S) There are only two possible causes of its squeaking: (1) he is playing with it; (2) he

---

[61] See a selection from *Summa Theologica*, reprinted in Hick (ed.), *The Existence of God*, p. 84. Compare with argument 330.

rolled on it in his sleep. If he rolled on it while sleeping he's awake now. Of course, if he is playing with his horse he's awake. So Mike must be awake now. (A)

($S, P = $ Mike is playing with the horse, $R = $ Mike rolled on the horse in his sleep, A)

145. Where in the body is hunger detected? The three classic answers are: (1) the stomach, (2) cells throughout the body, and (3) the brain.[62] Arguments 145 through 147 defend these views. The following argument summarizes the reasoning of A. J. Carlson.[63]

Whenever the empty stomach shows strong contractions, the subject invariably signals that he feels hunger. (W) If so, then the stomach is the basic source of hunger unless the central nervous system controls these contractions. A hungry dog whose stomach neural connections have been severed experiences stomach contractions. (D) This observation is incompatible with the thesis that stomach contractions are controlled by the central nervous system. Thus we have shown the stomach itself to be the basic source of hunger. (S)

($W, S, C = $ The central nervous system controls stomach contractions, D)

146. The French psychologist Joanny Roux reasoned this way in an 1897 paper:[64]

---

[62] For a detailed history of this problem see Mark R. Rosenzweig, "The Mechanisms of Hunger and Thirst," in *Psychology in the Making*, ed. by Leo Postman.

[63] *The Control of Hunger in Health and Disease.*

[64] "La Faim, Étude Physio-psychologique," *Bulletin de la Société d'Anthropologie de Lyon*, XVI (1897), 409–55. His view is explained in Rosenzweig, "The Mechanisms of Hunger and Thirst," pp. 96–97.

Hunger is caused either by the stomach or by the blood acting on the brain or by all the cells of the body. If the stomach causes hunger, then the removal of all the nerves connected to a rabbit's stomach will prevent normal eating. But doing this to a rabbit does not prevent normal eating. (R) Cerebral activity always starts with stimulation at the periphery. (P) If so, then hunger is not caused by the blood acting on the brain. It follows that hunger must be caused by all the cells of the body. (A)

(S = Hunger is caused by the stomach, B = Hunger is caused by the blood acting on the brain, A, R, P)

147. A number of contemporary scientists[65] have contributed to the following reasoning:

The brain is the cause of hunger, and the specific mechanism is the detection of the difference of glucose levels between arteries and veins. Proof: After one region of an animal's hypothalamus has been destroyed, the animal becomes obese. (O) When a different region in the hypothalamus has been destroyed, the animal ceases to eat. (C) Electrical stimulation of the hypothalamus can cause both eating and the cessation of eating. (E) All of these facts taken together mean that the brain is the cause of hunger. If the brain is the cause, then if glucose is the primary cell food the specific mechanism must be the detection of difference between arterial and venous glucose levels. Glucose is the main cell food. (G)

(B = The brain is the cause of hunger, M = The specific mechanism of hunger is the detection of the difference of glucose levels between arteries and veins, O, C, E, G)

148. The absent-minded professor has to locate his car by reasoning:

---

[65] See Rosenzweig, pp. 115–23.

I parked near Ashe, the library, or the School of Engineering. I parked at 1:00 p.m. and there are no empty parking spaces around Ashe at that time. If this is true, then I did not park near Ashe. If I parked near the engineering school I would remember the long walk; which I do not remember. So I must have parked beside the library. (L)

(A = I parked near Ashe, L, S = I parked near the School of Engineering, O = I parked at 1:00 p.m., E = There are empty parking spaces around Ashe at 1:00 p.m., R = I remember the long walk from the engineering school)

149. The *sense-datum theory*[66] maintains that what a person perceives directly are mental entities (sense data) rather than physical objects. One of the main arguments for the existence of sense data may be set out in this way:

I see a rose which appears pink to me. (A) The rose is red. (B) If I see a rose which appears pink to me, then there is something pink which I am seeing.[67] Now the rose can't be both red and pink. If there is something pink which I am seeing but the rose is not pink, then the rose is not the pink thing that I am seeing. If the rose isn't the pink thing that I am seeing, then there exists a pink sense datum which I am seeing. It follows that there is a pink sense datum which I am now seeing. (F)

(A, B, C = There is something pink which I am seeing, D = The rose is pink, E = The rose is the pink thing which I am seeing, F)

---

[66] For an introductory discussion of this and other theories in the philosophy of perception, see Fred A. Westphal, *The Activity of Philosophy*, pp. 233–52.

[67] This is a highly doubtful premise. See Winston H. F. Barnes, "The Myth of Sense-Data," *Proceedings of the Aristotelian Society*, XLV (1944–45), 89–117.

150. One way to prove that someone is advancing an invalid argument is to produce a second argument which has the same logical form as the first and which in addition has obviously true premises and an obviously false conclusion. The rationale of this procedure (which may be called "refutation by logical analogy") is set out by 150:

> Validity is wholly a matter of form. (F) Our two arguments have the same form. (S) If all of this is so, then your argument is valid if and only if mine is valid. My argument has true premises and a false conclusion. (A) It can't both have true premises and a false conclusion and be valid. So your argument is invalid. (Y)

$(F, S, Y, M = $ My argument is valid, $A)$

151. The verifiability criterion of meaning may be stated:

(C) A sentence is meaningful if and only if it is either analytic or verifiable.

An advocate of this criterion has difficulty explaining the status of C itself. This problem is pointed out succinctly by 151 and in more detail by 152.

> If C is true, it is meaningful. But also if it is true, then it isn't meaningful. Hence it isn't true. (T)

$(T, M = $ C is meaningful$)$

152. Every true statement is meaningful. (E) If this is so, then C is meaningful if it's true. If C is true, then it is meaningful if and only if it is either analytic or verifiable. But C is neither analytic nor verifiable. This proves that it isn't true. (T)

$(E, M = $ C is meaningful, $T, A = $ C is analytic, $V = $ C is verifiable$)$

153. Many people have puzzled over the fact that cigarette sales increased after the Surgeon General's report on smoking. Argument 153 attempts to explain this phenomenon (by deducing the statement which describes it from a set of true statements). The argument is an application of Leon Festinger's "Cognitive Dissonance" theory (see premise three).

Since publication of the Surgeon General's report nearly everyone believes that smoking is harmful. (R) It is inconsistent to (1) regard smoking as only moderately pleasurable, (2) believe that smoking is harmful, and (3) continue to smoke. (I) People struggle to avoid inconsistency. (S) If all the preceding assumptions are correct, then the individual smoker will either stop smoking or he will begin to regard smoking as providing great pleasure. It is easier to regard smoking as providing great pleasure than it is to stop smoking. (E) If this is so and if the individual smoker will either quit smoking or begin to regard smoking as extremely pleasurable, then the majority of smokers will come to regard smoking as providing great pleasure. If the majority of smokers come to regard smoking as highly pleasurable, then cigarette sales will increase. Thus cigarette sales will increase. (C)

$(R, I, S, X = $ The individual smoker will either stop smoking or he will begin to regard smoking as providing great pleasure,[68] $E, M = $ The majority of smokers will come to regard smoking as providing great pleasure, C)

154. *Psychological egoism* is the view that all people *always* act in their own self-interest. Argument 154 is an attack on this theory.

If the thesis of psychological egoism is synthetic (that is, factual), then there is evidence which counts against it. If it is syn-

---

[68] Contrary to appearances, this statement (X) is not a truth-functional disjunction.

thetic and there is evidence which counts against it, then it is false. If, on the other hand, the thesis is analytic (that is, true by definition), then it is empty. The thesis must be either analytic or synthetic. So it must be either false or empty.

(S = The thesis of psychological egoism is synthetic, C = There is evidence which counts against it, F = The thesis is false, A = The thesis is analytic, E = The thesis is empty)

155. A gasoline company executive advanced the following argument during congressional hearings on the "games" and contests sponsored by petroleum companies.

> (Because of the popularity of the games) one gasoline company cannot stop sponsoring the games unless they all stop. All of the companies will stop only if they agree among themselves to stop or if they are forced to stop by the federal government. The companies cannot agree among themselves to stop without violating anti-trust laws. Therefore unless the gas companies violate anti-trust laws, the federal government's forcing all of the companies to quit the games is a necessary condition for even one company's cancelling its game.

(O = One gasoline company stops its game, A = All gasoline companies stop their games, B = All the gasoline companies agree among themselves to stop their games, F = The federal government forces all gasoline companies to stop their games, V = The gasoline companies violate anti-trust laws)

156. The *ontological argument* for the existence of God was advanced by St. Anselm in the eleventh century. Anselm presented two versions of this argument. The first[69] may be formalized:

---

[69] This version appears in chapter two of Anselm's *Proslogion.* See Hick, ed., *The Existence of God,* pp. 25–26.

God is a being a greater than which cannot be conceived. (G) We understand the term 'God.' (U) If we understand this term, then God exists in the understanding. If God exists in the understanding but not in reality, then we can conceive of a being greater than God (namely, a being who is like God except that he exists both in the understanding and in reality). Our conceiving of a being which is greater than God would show that God is not a being a greater than which cannot be conceived. It follows that God exists in reality. (R)

(G = God is a being a greater than which cannot be conceived, U, A = God exists in the understanding, R, C = We can conceive of a being greater than God)

157. The second form of Anselm's argument:[70]

God is a being a greater than which cannot be conceived. (G) It is possible to conceive of a being which cannot be conceived not to exist. (P) If this is possible and if God can be conceived not to exist, then we can conceive of a being which is greater than God. But if we can conceive of a being greater than God, God is not a being a greater than which cannot be conceived. If God cannot be conceived not to exist, then he must exist. Thus God exists. (E)

(G, P, A = God can be conceived not to exist, C = We can conceive of a being greater than God, E)

158. The philosopher Norman Malcolm has expanded Anselm's second version of the ontological argument.[71]

[70] See chapter three of *Proslogion* in Hick, ed., *The Existence of God*, pp. 26–27.
[71] See Malcolm's "Anselm's Ontological Arguments," *The Philosophical Review*, LXIX (1960), 41–62.

God is a being a greater than which cannot be conceived. (G) If God is dependent upon something for his existence, then we can conceive of a being which is greater than God (namely, a being who is like God except that he is not dependent upon anything for his existence). Conceiving of a being greater than God would prove that God is not a being a greater than which cannot be conceived. If God can either come into existence or can pass out of existence, then he is dependent upon something for his existence. If God exists and he cannot pass out of existence, then his existence is necessary. On the other hand, if God does not exist and he cannot come into existence, then his existence is impossible. God's existence is not impossible unless the concept of "God" is contradictory. But that concept is not contradictory. Therefore God's existence is necessary. (N)

(G, D = God is dependent upon something for his existence, C = We can conceive of a being which is greater than God, A = God can come into existence, B = God can pass out of existence, E = God exists, N, I = God's existence is impossible, F = The concept of "God" is contradictory)

159. One of the classic criticisms of the ontological argument was formulated by Kant.[72] Argument 159 paraphrases this criticism:

The ontological argument treats existence as a perfection. (A) If this is true, then it is a cogent argument only if existence actually is a perfection. Perfections are properties. (E) If so, then existence is not a perfection unless it is a property. If existence is a property, then a real dollar possesses some characteristic which a merely possible dollar lacks. However, a real dollar does not exhibit any characteristics which a merely possible dollar lacks. (D) Hence the ontological argument is not cogent. (C)

---

[72] See *Critique of Pure Reason*, pp. 500–507.

(A, C, B = Existence is a perfection, E, F = Existence is a property, D = A real dollar exhibits some characteristic which a merely possible dollar lacks)

160. $2 = 1 + 1$. (A) $3 = 2 + 1$. (B) $4 = 3 + 1$. (C) Addition is associative. (D) $4 = 4$. (E) If $4 = 4$ and $4 = 3 + 1$, then $3 + 1 = 4$. If $3 + 1 = 4$ and $3 = 2 + 1$, then $(2 + 1) + 1 = 4$. If addition is associative, then $(2 + 1) + 1 = 4$ if and only if $2 + (1 + 1) = 4$. If $2 + (1 + 1) = 4$ and $2 = 1 + 1$, then $2 + 2 = 4$. This proves that $2 + 2 = 4$. (J)

(A, B, C, D, E, $F = 3 + 1 = 4$, $G = (2 + 1) + 1 = 4$, $H = 2 + (1 + 1) = 4$, J)

161. Many logicians maintain that argument 258 is invalid:

(P) All Lutherans are Protestants.

(C) Therefore some Lutherans are Protestants.

On the surface, 258 appears to be a sound inference. Arguments 161 and 162 reflect the reasoning which logicians employ in classifying 258 invalid. (Note that one can avoid accepting the conclusion of 162 by rejecting the first or third premise of 161.)

P means 'There are no Lutherans who aren't Protestants.' (A) If P means this and there are no Lutherans, then P is true. C means 'There is at least one Lutheran who is a Protestant.' (B) If C means this, then if there aren't any Lutherans C will be false. Therefore if there are no Lutherans, P is true and C false.

(A, L = There exists at least one Lutheran, T = P is true, B, F = C is false)

162.   It is logically possible that there are no Lutherans. (X) If there are no Lutherans, P is true and C false. If all of the preceding is so, then it is logically possible that P is true and C false. Argument 258 is valid if and only if it is logically impossible that P is true and C false. Hence 258 is invalid. (V)

(X = It is logically possible that there are no Lutherans, L = There exists at least one Lutheran, T = P is true, F = C is false, Y = It is logically possible that P is true and C false, V)

163.   If Goodman knew about Clark's article on *The Structure of Appearance* and considered the article significant, then he would have referred to it in the second edition. There is no reference to the article in the second edition. (R) So either Goodman did not know of the article's existence or he did know but did not consider it a significant article.

(K = Goodman knew about Clark's article, S = Goodman considered the article significant, R)

164. A *Monitor* reporter questioned students at the University of West Virginia on the topic "Should the United States continue to support its space program?" Answers given by two students are paraphrased by 164 and 165.

     Eliminating hunger and slums should have priority over exploring the moon. (E) If this is true, then we ought to spend money on the space program only if both of the following conditions are met: (1) it is possible to finance rocketry, butter, and slum clearance at the same time, and (2) we are waging an all-out war on hunger and slums. Since we are not at present waging total war on either hunger or slums, it is false that we ought to be spending money on the U. S. space effort.

(E, O = We ought to spend money on the U. S. space program, P = It is possible to finance rocketry, butter, and slum clearance at the same time, H = We are waging an all-out war on hunger, S = We are waging an all-out war on slums)

165.   By the year 2000 there will be more humans than the earth can accommodate. (B) If so, then we ought to colonize the moon. We will not colonize the moon without perfecting space transportation. We cannot perfect space transportation unless we support the U. S. space program. If we ought to colonize the moon, and if supporting the U. S. space program is a necessary condition for colonizing the moon, then we ought to spend money on the U. S. space effort. It follows that we ought to support the nation's space effort. (E)

(B, A = We *ought* to colonize the moon, C = We *do* colonize the moon, P = We perfect space transportation, D = We *do* support the U. S. space program, E = We *ought* to support the U. S. space effort) Distinguish between statements A and C, and between statements D and E.

166. The English scientist Karl Pearson believed that mental characteristics were almost entirely hereditary. He supported his view in a 1904 article[73] with the following chain of reasoning.

The degree of resemblance in physical characteristics between siblings exactly matches the degree of resemblance in mental characteristics. (A) If this is true, then the amount of environmental influence in the one area will equal the amount in the other. If environmental factors have any significant influence

---

[73] "On the Laws of Inheritance of Man," *Biometrika*, III (1904), 131–90.

in the physical realm, then they will influence eye color. But they don't influence eye color. (D) If the amount of environmental influence in the physical realm equals the amount in the mental realm, then environmental factors are significant in the former area if and only if they are significant in the latter. Therefore environmental factors are not significant in the determination of mental characteristics. (E)

(A, B = The amount of environmental influence in the physical area equals the amount in the mental area, C = Environmental factors are significant in the determination of physical characteristics, D, E)

167. How are 'only if' sentences to be translated into standard form? Should S1 be translated as S2 or S3?

    (S1) p only if q
    (S2)   if q, then p
    (S3)   if p, then q

Argument 167 gives an answer to this question.

    S1 is equivalent to 'if not q, then not p.' (A) The latter is equivalent to S3. (B) If all of this is so, then S1 and S3 are equivalent. S2 is not equivalent to S3. (D) If S2 isn't equivalent to S3, then it can't both be the case that S1 is equivalent to S2 and also to S3. This proves that S1 is equivalent to S3, and not to S2.

(A, B, C = S1 is equivalent to S3, D, E = S1 is equivalent to S2)

168. There are other ways of arguing that 'p only if q' should not be translated as 'if q, then p,' for example, 168. Consider these six statement-forms:

(S1) *p* only if *q*
(S2) if *q*, then *p*
(S3) *p* if *q*
(S4) *p* if *q*, and *p* only if *q*
(S5) *p* if *q*, and *p* if *q*
(S6) *p* if and only if *q*

The reasoning:

S2 and S3 are logically equivalent. (A) If S1 is logically equivalent to S2 and S2 to S3, then S1 and S3 are logically equivalent. If S1 and S3 are equivalent, then so also are S4 and S5. S3 and S5 are equivalent. (E) If S3 and S5 are equivalent and S4 and S5 are equivalent, then S3 and S4 are. S4 is equivalent to S6. (G) If S3 is equivalent to S4 and S4 to S6, then S3 and S6 are logically equivalent. However, S3 is not equivalent to S6. (H) It follows that S1 is not logically equivalent to S2. (B)

(A, B, C = S1 and S3 are logically equivalent, D = S4 and S5 are logically equivalent, E, F = S3 and S4 are logically equivalent, G, H)

169. If evolutionary theory is correct, then there exists an ancestral chain which leads from me back to some very primitive organism (call it "a"). This "a" did not survive its death. (A) If there is an ancestral chain linking me to "a," then if "a" did not survive its death but I shall survive mine, somewhere in the chain there was an animal which survived death even though neither of its parents did. Now it seems absurd to hold that there was an animal in the chain which survived death while its parents did not. (B) So either evolutionary theory is wrong or I will not survive death.

(E = Evolutionary theory is correct, C = There exists an ancestral chain linking me to "a," A, I = I shall survive death, B = Somewhere in the chain was an animal which survived death while its parents did not)

170. The following puzzle appears in *101 Puzzles in Thought and Logic* by C. R. Wylie, Jr.:[74]

> During a call that I once paid young Mrs. Addlepate I was introduced to her three charming children. By way of making conversation I inquired their ages.
>
> "I can't remember exactly," my hostess replied with a smile, "I'm no good at figures. But if Bill isn't the youngest then I guess Alice is, and if Carl isn't the youngest then Alice is the oldest. Does that help?"
>
> I said that of course it did, although it really didn't at all until days later when it suddenly dawned on me that although Mrs. Addlepate hadn't been able to tell me the ages of her children I could at least tell from her curious remarks which one was the oldest, the next oldest, and the youngest.
>
> What were the relative ages of the three children?

(Read no further if you want to attack the problem on your own.) The answer to the puzzle is contained in the conclusion of 170; the premises give a compressed version of the solution. The first and third premises are stated in the puzzle; the second, fourth, and fifth are obvious truths.

> **If Bill isn't the youngest, then Alice is. If either Bill or Alice is youngest, then Carl isn't youngest. If Carl isn't the youngest, then Alice is the oldest. Alice cannot be both oldest and youngest. If Alice is oldest and Bill youngest, then Carl must be next to the oldest. It follows that Alice is the oldest, Carl the next oldest, and Bill the youngest.**

[74] Dover Publications, Inc., New York, 1957, puzzle 22. Reprinted through permission of the publisher.

(B = Bill is the youngest, A = Alice is the youngest, C = Carl is the youngest, O = Alice is the oldest, N = Carl is the next oldest)

171. A senior education major submitted a term paper in American philosophy which was crammed with stylistic errors. I confronted him with 171.

> If you permit your future students to get away with errors like these, then you will be helping to give them an inferior education. If, on the other hand, you won't let them get away with errors of this sort and yet you continue to make them yourself, you will be applying to them standards which you do not apply to yourself. If you apply standards to them which you won't adopt for yourself, you will be inconsistent. Therefore if you continue to make these kinds of errors yourself you will either be helping to give your students a poor education or you will be inconsistent.

(P = You permit your future students to get away with errors like these, H = You help to give these students an inferior education, C = You continue to make errors of this sort, S = You apply standards to your students which you do not apply to yourself, I = You will be inconsistent)

172. In "The Dilemma of Determinism," [75] William James draws out some unfortunate consequences of determinism. Argument 172 paraphrases his reasoning.

> Murders are committed and regretted. If murder is not bad, then judgments of regret are incorrect. If determinism is true, then if murders occur and are bad, sin is a necessary part of the world. If determinism is correct, then if murders are regretted and judgments of regret are mistaken, error is a necessary feature of the

---

[75] In *Essays in Pragmatism*, p. 50.

world. Hence if determinism is correct, then either sin or error is a necessary part of the world.

(C = Murders are committed, R = Murders are regretted, B = Murders are bad, J = Judgments of regret are correct, D = Determinism is correct, S = Sin is a necessary part of the world, E = Error is a necessary part of the world)

173. Some universities have recently adopted the following policy concerning the travel expenses of persons interviewed for faculty vacancies:

> The school pays if and only if it is not the case both that the school makes an offer and that the applicant refuses the job.

Argument 173 reveals the rationale for such a policy.

> The school pays if and only if it is not the case both that the school makes an offer and that the applicant refuses the job. If not offering the job is a sufficient condition for the school's paying, then the policy discourages the school from interviewing persons the school is not genuinely interested in hiring. If the job's being offered and turned down is a sufficient condition for the school's not paying, then the policy discourages applicants who are not genuinely interested in the job from interviewing. Therefore the policy discourages the school from interviewing a person in whom it is not genuinely interested and it also discourages applicants not really interested in the school from interviewing.

(P = The school pays, O = The school makes an offer, R = The applicant refuses the job, A = The policy discourages the school from interviewing persons they are not genuinely interested in, B = The policy discourages applicants not genuinely interested in the job from interviewing)

174. Consider these sentences:

(A) All racists are insecure.

(O) Some racists are not insecure.

Some logicians have said the following about A and O:

A means 'There are racists and each racist is insecure.'

O means 'There are racists and some of them are not insecure.'

A and O are contradictories.

This position is logically inconsistent. Argument 174 shows this by deriving a contradiction from these sentences (with the help of supplementary premises).

> A means 'There are racists and each racist is insecure.' (B) O means 'There are racists and some of them are not insecure.' (D) A and O are contradictories. (C) If it is logically possible for A and O both to be false, then they aren't contradictories. It is logically possible that there are no racists. (X) If racists don't exist and A means 'There are racists and each racist is insecure,' then A is false. If there are no racists and O means 'There are racists and some of them are not insecure,' then O is false. If (1) it is logically possible that there aren't any racists and (2) A and O are false if there are no racists, then it is logically possible that A and O are both false. So A and O both are and are not contradictories.

(*B, D, C, W* = It is logically possible for A and O both to be false, *X, R* = There exists at least one racist, *Y* = A is false, *Z* = O is false)

175. The method of conditional proof permits one to prove indirectly that an argument of the form A1 is valid by demonstrating the validity of an argument of the form A2:

> (A1) B.
> _____
> Therefore if C, then D.
>
> (A2) B.
> C.
> _____
> Therefore D.

Corresponding to arguments A1 and A2, respectively, are statements S1 and S2:

> (S1) If B, then if C then D.
> (S2) If both B and C, then D.

The following argument is a justification of the method of conditional proof:

> A1 is valid if and only if S1 is a logical truth. A2 is valid if and only if S2 is a logical truth. S1 and S2 are logically equivalent. (*I*) If this is so, then if either is logically true then both are. Conclusion: A1 is valid if and only if A2 is valid.

($E = $ A1 is valid, $F = $ S1 is a logical truth, $G = $ A2 is valid, $H = $ S2 is a logical truth, I)

176. If to every significant grammatical subject there corresponds some object which it denotes, then the expression 'the class of all classes which are not members of themselves' is a significant grammatical subject only if it denotes something. That expression *is* a significant grammatical subject. (*S*) A necessary condition for that expression's denoting something is the existence of the class of all classes which are not members of themselves. If there is such a class, then (1) if it is a member of itself then it is not a member of itself, and (2) if it is not a member of itself then it must be a member of itself. This proves the falsity of the thesis that to every significant grammatical subject there corresponds an object which it denotes. (C) [76]

(C, S, D = The expression 'the class . . . themselves' denotes something, E = There exists a class of all classes which are not members of themselves, M = The class of all classes which are not members of themselves is a member of itself)

177. Mathematical reasoning is deductive. Consider for example the following geometric proof that the sum of the interior angles of a triangle is 180°.

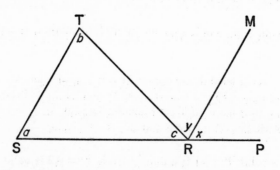

(By construction) RM and ST are parallel lines. (P)

(By construction) SP is a straight line. (S)

---

[76] Gilbert Ryle advances this argument in "The Theory of Meaning," in *British Philosophy in the Mid-Century*, ed. by C. A. Mace, pp. 252–53. The argument employs Russell's paradox concerning the class of all classes which are not members of themselves. For a discussion of this and other paradoxes see W. V. Quine, "Paradox," *Scientific American*, CCVI (April, 1962), 84–96.

The corresponding angles formed when two parallel lines are cut by a transversal are equal. (C)

If all of the preceding is so, then angles a and x are equal.

The alternate interior angles formed when two parallel lines are cut by a transversal are equal. (A)

If this is so, then if RM and ST are parallel, then angles b and y are equal.

If SP is a straight line, then the sum of the angles c, y, and x is 180°.

If the sum of the angles c, y, and x is 180° and a and x are equal and b and y are equal, then the sum of the interior angles of triangle STR is 180°.

We have stipulated neither the size nor the shape of triangle STR.

If this is so and if the sum of the interior angles of triangle STR is 180°, then the sum of the interior angles of any plane triangle is 180°.

Therefore the sum of the interior angles of any plane triangle is 180°. (X)

(P, S, C, Q = Angles a and x are equal, A, R = Angles b and y are equal, T = The sum of the angles c, y, and x is 180°, U = The sum of the interior angles of triangle STR is 180°, V = We have stipulated the size of triangle STR, W = We have stipulated the shape of triangle STR, X)

178. (DIFFICULT) While a graduate student at M. I. T. in the late thirties, Claude Shannon discovered a remarkable parallel between electric switching circuits and truth-functional logic.[77] He found that a circuit can be represented by a logical formula in which (1)

---

[77] See Shannon, "A Symbolic Analysis of Relay and Switching Circuits," *Transactions of the American Institute of Electrical Engineers,* LVII (1938), 713–23.

statement letters and their negations stand for switch positions, (2) the series connection of components is represented by conjunction, and (3) the parallel connection of components is represented by disjunction (or alternation). On the basis of this correspondence one can simplify a switching circuit by means of the following steps:

(1) Represent the circuit by a logical formula.

(2) By logical techniques replace this formula by a second one which is simpler, yet logically equivalent to it.

(3) Translate the second formula into circuitry.

Consider an example:

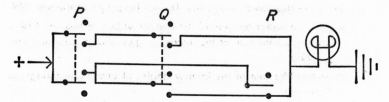

This circuit (C1) can be represented by formula F1:

(F1) Either both not *P* and not *Q*, or both *P* and either not *Q* or not *R*.

F1 is logically equivalent to the simpler formula F2:

(F2) Either not *Q* or both *P* and not *R*.

F2 translates into circuitry as C2:

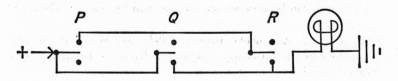

These two electric circuits are functionally equivalent (that is, they do the same job), yet C2 has only three switch components while C1 has five.

One claim in this account needs support—the claim that F1 and F2 are logically equivalent. They are equivalent if and only if F1 entails F2 (argument 178) and F2 entails F1 (179). Check the validity of these arguments.

> **F1. So F2.**

(P, Q, R)

179. (DIFFICULT)

> **F2. So F1.**

(See 178.)

180. (DIFFICULT) *Time*[78] gives the following account of a wild art auction which took place in 1965 at Christie's of London:

> . . . Bidding started at $294,000, then leaped first by $1,500 bounds, then by $3,000, then by $30,000. It was a three-way race until Agnew's of London dropped out at $2,116,800, and from then on the bidding see-sawed between Marlborough Fine Arts, Ltd. . . . and Norton Simon, the California industrialist and art collector. . . . Finally the price leveled at $2,175,000. Four times Christie's auctioneer, I. O. Chance, repeated the bid; then he brought down his hammer, announced:

---

[78] See "The Market: Son of Rembrandt," *Time*, March 26, 1965, p. 70. Copyright Time, Inc., 1965.

"Sold to Marlborough Fine Arts." Applause scattered across the room for what seemed to be the Rembrandt's retention by the British. Then it abruptly stopped.

. . . Simon had sprung to his feet. "I have not finished bidding," he protested.

For a moment Auctioneer Chance was speechless. Then: "What did you say?"

"I said I hadn't finished bidding," said Simon. "You got my message. I am still bidding."

To prove it, Simon extricated from his U. S. passport a copy of his agreement with Christie's. He opened the paper, pointed to it and read: "When Mr. Simon is sitting down, he is bidding. If he bids openly, he is also bidding. When he stands up, he has stopped bidding. If he sits down again, he is not bidding unless he raises his finger. Having raised his finger, he is bidding, until he stands up again."

In 31 years of auctioning, Chance had never faced such confusion. However, Christie's catalogue for the sale clearly stated, "if any dispute arises between two or more Bidders, the Lot so in dispute shall be immediately put up again and re-sold." As bedlam took over, Chance declared: "I have no option but to reopen the bidding." In a matter of seconds, with Marlborough no longer interested, Rembrandt's *Titus* became Simon's. The price: $2,234,400. . . .

Had Simon employed a little logic, he could have put his instructions in a much less confusing way. (Of course, he may have *intended* to confuse the auctioneer.) Leaving out the superfluous statement regarding open bidding, Simon's instructions can be paraphrased by the following four sentences:

(S1) If Simon is sitting and he has not previously stood, then he is bidding.

(S2) If Simon is standing, then he is not bidding.

(S3) If Simon is sitting and has previously stood, then he is not bidding unless he has raised his finger.

(S4) If Simon is sitting and has previously stood, then he is bidding if he has raised his finger.

Now, these four sentences taken together are logically equivalent to (that is, say exactly the same thing as) the following sentence:

(S5) Simon is bidding if and only if he is sitting and either has not previously stood or has raised his finger.

We can prove that S5 is logically equivalent to the set S1 through S4 by showing that S5 entails each of those sentences (arguments 180 through 183) and that those four sentences together entail S5 (184). If all five arguments are valid, then we know S5 to be equivalent to Simon's actual instructions.

S5. Therefore S1.

(B = Simon is bidding, S = Simon is sitting, P = Simon has previously stood, R = Simon has raised his finger)

181. (DIFFICULT)

S5. Therefore S2.

(See 180.)

182. (DIFFICULT)

S5. Therefore S3.

(See 180.)

183. (DIFFICULT)

> S5. Therefore S4.

(See 180.)

184. (DIFFICULT)

> S1. S2. S3. S4. Therefore S5.

(See 180.)

185. (DIFFICULT) The syndicated sports columnist Robert Lipsyte writes:[79]

> The Lakers win when Chamberlain or Baylor or West gets hot, or any two of the three do well. The Celtics win when the running game works. . . .

Add to this passage the obvious truth that if the Lakers play the Celtics, then it is not the case that both teams win. Does the resulting set of statements entail the following proposition?

> If the Lakers play the Celtics and the Celtics' running game works, then none of the three men, Chamberlain, Baylor, West, is hot, and at most one of them does well.

(L = The Lakers win, D = Chamberlain gets hot, E = Baylor gets hot, F = West gets hot, G = Chamberlain does well, H = Baylor does well, I = West does well, C = The Celtics win, R = The Celtics' running game works, P = The Lakers play the Celtics)

---

[79] "Logic Ends When It's Wilt Vs. Russell," *The Miami News*, April 28, 1969, p. 3–B. © 1969 by The New York Times Company. Reprinted by permission.

4 | Valid Nonrelational Quantificational Arguments

186. Anyone who deliberates about alternative courses of action believes he is free. Everybody deliberates about alternative courses of action. So we all believe ourselves to be free.[80]

(Universe of discourse:[81] persons; $Dx = x$ deliberates about alternative courses of action, $Bx = x$ believes himself to be free)

187. All arguments which beg the question are valid. Proof: An argument begs the question if and only if it has a premise which by itself entails the argument's conclusion.[82] Every argument having a premise which by itself entails the conclusion of the argument is valid.

(Universe of discourse: arguments; $Bx = x$ begs the question, $Vx = x$ is valid, $Ex = x$ has a premise which by itself entails the conclusion of x)

---

[80] See James W. Cornman and Keith Lehrer, *Philosophical Problems and Arguments: An Introduction*, pp. 131–41.

[81] See convention four in *Student's Preface*.

[82] Argument 335 casts doubt on this premise.

188. In 1954 in the case of "Brown versus the Board of Education of Topeka," the Supreme Court ruled unanimously that school segregation was unconstitutional. The heart of the reasoning contained in their opinion is represented by 188.

All school segregation generates feelings of inferiority among members of the minority group. Any school segregation which does this treats students unequally. Any school segregation which treats students unequally violates the Fourteenth Amendment. Hence any instance of school segregation is a violation of this Amendment.

(Universe of discourse: instances of school segregation; $Gx = x$ generates inferiority feelings among the minority group, $Ux = x$ treats students unequally, $Vx = x$ violates the Fourteenth Amendment)

189. The philosophers S. I. Benn and R. S. Peters maintain that causal explanations are inadequate for much human behavior.[83] Argument 189 paraphrases one of their reasons.

Some human behavior is rule following. Rule-following behavior cannot be explained adequately in terms of causes. Consequently some human behavior cannot be adequately explained causally.

(Universe of discourse: human behavior; $Rx = x$ is rule following, $Cx = x$ can be adequately explained causally)

190. Does the sentence 'Either it is raining or it is not raining' say anything (that is, have content)? Call the sentence 'S.'

---

[83] See chapter nine of *Social Principles and the Democratic State*.

Anything S says has to do with the weather. S doesn't say anything about the weather. So S doesn't say anything at all.

($Sx = x$ is stated by S, $Wx = x$ is about the weather)

191. During a one-day law-enforcement conference police cruisers were parked all over the campus. Many were parked by "NO PARKING" signs, and in "STICKER ONLY" lots. A philosophy graduate student (Rocky Walters; see argument 1) tried, without success, to get the campus police to issue parking tickets to the lawmen. Rocky's argument:

The law applies to everyone. Therefore the law applies to all policemen.

(Universe of discourse: persons; $Lx = $ the law applies to x, $Px = x$ is a policeman)

192. Students should not *control* the hiring of any faculty members. Hence they should not control the hiring of teachers in the Department of Black Studies.

(Universe of discourse: faculty members; $Hx = $ the hiring of x should be under the control of students, $Bx = x$ is in the Department of Black Studies)

193. There are people who publicly praise law and order while privately encouraging defiance of law. Anyone who praises law and order in public but encourages violation of the law in private is contemptible. So some of those who publicly sing the praises of law and order are contemptible people.

(Universe of discourse: persons; $Px = x$ praises law and order publicly, $Ex = x$ encourages defiance of law privately, $Cx = x$ is contemptible)

194. In *The Foundations of Scientific Inference*,[84] Wesley Salmon sums up a line of reasoning with the following argument:

> . . . If an ampliative inference could be justified deductively it would not be ampliative. It follows that ampliative inference cannot be justified deductively.

By "ampliative inference," Salmon means an inference whose conclusion has content not found in its premises. Prove the validity of Salmon's argument. (Universe of discourse: inferences; $Ax = x$ is ampliative, $Dx = x$ can be justified deductively)

195.   Members of the electoral college are either useless or dangerous. The reason: they are useless if they do their job and dangerous if they don't.

(Universe of discourse: members of the electoral college; $Ux = x$ is useless, $Dx = x$ is dangerous, $Jx = x$ does his job)

196.   The denial that there are propositions is itself a proposition. Hence propositions exist.[85]

($d =$ the denial that there are propositions, $Px = x$ is a proposition)

197.   This logic book doesn't contain a single example from Lewis Carroll. So it is false that every logic book has examples taken from Carroll's works.

(Universe of discourse: logic books; $t =$ this book, $Cx = x$ has examples from Lewis Carroll)

---

[84] P. 11.
[85] This argument is advanced by Frederic Fitch in "The Reality of Propositions," *The Review of Metaphysics*, IX (1955), 3.

198.   Every event is caused. No caused event is free. Therefore no human acts are free.

(Universe of discourse: events; $Cx = x$ is caused, $Fx = x$ is free, $Hx = x$ is a human act)

199. Add 'There are prepositions' to the premise set of 10.

(Px, Mx, Nx)

200. Is the following sentence analytic?

(S) The word 'cat' exists.

Argument 200 attempts to prove that S is not analytic, and 201 seeks to prove that it is analytic. (At least one of the arguments must contain a false premise.)

No existential sentence is analytic. S is an existential sentence. So it can't be analytic.

(Universe of discourse: sentences; Ex, Ax, s = sentence S)

201.   Any sentence which can be known to be true solely on the basis of understanding it, is a priori. Only analytic sentences are a priori. S can be known to be true merely on the basis of understanding it. Hence S is analytic.

(Universe of discourse: sentences; $Ux = x$ can be known to be true solely on the basis of understanding it, $Bx = x$ is a priori, $Cx = x$ is analytic, s = sentence S)

202.   Mental events are not brain events. The proof: Mental events are private. Brain events are physical. Physical events are public. Public events aren't private. Q.E.D.

($Mx = x$ is a mental event, $Bx = x$ is a brain event, $Ax = x$ is a private event, $Cx = x$ is a physical event, $Dx = x$ is a public event)

203. Logic texts commonly say that *any* argument having the form 'If p then q; q; therefore p' (affirming the consequent) is invalid. This is a mistake; some arguments which have this form are valid. Argument 203 is an example.[86]

       If something is red, everything is red. Everything is red. Therefore something is red.

($Rx = x$ is red)

204.   Argument 203 affirms the consequent; nevertheless it is valid. So it is false that all arguments which affirm the consequent are invalid.

(Universe of discourse: arguments; o = argument 203, $Ax = x$ affirms the consequent, $Vx = x$ is valid)

205. The students in Dr. Westphal's introduction to philosophy class did so poorly on the mid-term exam that he made this unusual proposal to them: Any student who wishes to may take a make-up test and the higher of his two grades will be recorded. A poor turn-out for the make-up exam provoked the following inference:

---

[86] For a discussion of this mistake and similar ones see James Willard Oliver, "Formal Fallacies and Other Invalid Arguments," *Mind*, LXXVI (1967), 463–78. Argument 203 is Oliver's example.

Anyone who fails to take the make-up is a fool unless he got an "A" on the mid-term. Some students in the class who did not receive "A"s on the mid-term did not take the make-up test. Hence there are fools in the class.

(Universe of discourse: students in Westphal's class; $Mx = x$ takes the make-up test, $Ax = x$ got an "A" on the mid-term test, $Fx = x$ is a fool)

206. I Kings, chapter 18 (verses 20 to 40) describes a contest on Mt. Carmel between Elijah and 450 prophets of Baal. Elijah regards the result of the contest as a demonstration of the divinity of Jehovah. His reasoning:

A god is God if and only if he answers his prophets by fire. Jehovah answers by fire, but Baal doesn't. Therefore Jehovah is God and Baal is not.

(Universe of discourse: gods; $Gx = x$ is God, $Fx = x$ answers his prophets by fire, $j =$ Jehovah, $b =$ Baal)

207. Kant advances the following argument in *Foundations of the Metaphysics of Morals*:[87]

Every duty is either rigorous or meritorious. All rigorous duties follow from the categorical imperative, and so do all meritorious duties. Thus all duties follow from the categorical imperative.

(Universe of discourse: duties; Rx, Mx, $Cx = x$ follows from the categorical imperative)

---

[87] P. 42.

208. Argument 69 was an attack on the thesis that scientific laws are prescriptions or rules. Argument 208 criticizes the thesis in another way.

Rules are neither true nor false. Scientific laws are true. So scientific laws are not rules.

($Rx = x$ is a rule, $Tx = x$ is true, $Fx = x$ is false, $Sx = x$ is a scientific law)

209. If the following syllogism is tested with one of the standard techniques of syllogistic logic (the Venn diagram test, for example) it will be judged invalid.[88] It commits the "fallacy" of drawing an affirmative conclusion from a negative premise. Quantificational logic permits a deeper analysis of the argument; such analysis shows the argument to be valid. Can you spot the peculiar characteristic of the argument which guarantees its validity? (Hint: See 53.)

Some tall men are not mortal. All men are mortal. Therefore all men are tall men.

(Universe of discourse: men; $Tx = x$ is tall, $Mx = x$ is mortal)

210. Any argument which has a logically contradictory premise set is valid. The first premise of 209 entails 'Some men are not mortal.' (E) 'Some men are not mortal' is the denial of the second premise of 209. (D) [89] If the first premise entails 'Some men are not mortal' and if that sentence is the denial of the second prem-

---

[88] Argument 209 is based on an example given by Oliver in "Formal Fallacies . . . ," p. 472.

[89] 'E' and 'D' are symbols from truth-functional logic; they represent statements.

ise, then the premise set of 209 is logically contradictory. It
follows that argument 209 is valid.

(Universe of discourse: arguments; $Cx = x$ has a logically contradictory premise set, Vx, E, D, a = argument 209)

211. A second example of a valid argument which will test out "invalid" under the techniques of syllogistic logic:

> No men are immortal. No tall men are immortal. So all tall
> men are men.

Exercise 315 may help you see why this unpersuasive argument is
formally valid. ($Mx = x$ is a man, $Ix = x$ is immortal, $Tx = x$ is tall)

212. In *An Essay Concerning Human Understanding*, John Locke
advances many arguments intended to downgrade the importance
of syllogistic reasoning.[90] For example:

> If syllogisms are the only proper instrument of reason, then
> no man before Aristotle knew anything by reason. However, obvi-
> ously, there were men before Aristotle's time who knew things by
> reason. Hence some proper instruments of reasoning are nonsyl-
> logistic.

($Sx = x$ is a syllogism, $Px = x$ is a proper instrument of reason,
$Ax = x$ is a man who lived before the time of Aristotle, $Kx = x$ knows
some things by reason)

213.   No musical composition exhibits complete irregularity.
Reason: If the composition contains any repeated sequences, regu-

---

[90] See II, 388–405.

larity is present; and if no sequence is ever repeated, then this fact itself constitutes a notable regularity.[91]

(Universe of discourse: musical compositions; $Sx = x$ contains some repetition, $Rx = x$ exhibits some regularity)

214. Logic students sometimes doubt the claim that all conditional sentences (sentences of the form "if p then q") with false antecedents (the "p" part) are true.[92] Argument 214 shows that this claim is a logical consequence of the standard ascription of truth conditions to the conditional, taken together with an obvious logical truth.

A conditional is true if and only if it does not have a true antecedent and a false consequent. No conditionals with false antecedents have true antecedents. Therefore all conditionals with false antecedents are true.

(Universe of discourse: conditionals; $Jx = x$ is true, $Kx = x$ has a true antecedent, $Lx = x$ has a false consequent, $Mx = x$ has a false antecedent)

215.   If God has foreknowledge of everything, then no person has free will. Consequently God cannot have both foreknowledge of everything and free will.

(Universe of discourse: persons; $g =$ God, $Kx = x$ has foreknowledge of everything, $Wx = x$ has free will)

216. The University of Miami recently adopted a voluntary-attend-

---

[91] Nelson Goodman advances this reasoning in "Art and Inquiry," *Proceedings and Addresses of the American Philosophical Association*, XLI (1968), p. 17.

[92] Their doubt may be correct; see 236.

ance policy. As 216 indicates, this policy prohibits teachers from employing a certain type of pop-quiz policy.

> (The attendance policy specifies that) no teacher will penalize students for cutting on nonexam days. Any teacher who gives pop quizzes and does not excuse students who cut on days when pops are administered is penalizing his students for cutting on nonexam days. Therefore if a teacher gives pop quizzes he will excuse students who cut on days when the pops are given.

(Universe of discourse: teachers; $Px = x$ penalizes students for cutting on nonexam days, $Gx = x$ gives pop quizzes, $Ex = x$ excuses students who cut on days when pop quizzes are given)

217. If a University of Miami teacher gives pop quizzes he will excuse students who cut on days when the pops are given. If a UM teacher who gives pop quizzes excuses students who cut on days when the pops are administered, then he penalizes those students who attend class. So any UM teacher who gives pop quizzes penalizes those students who attend his class.

(Universe of discourse: UM teachers; $Gx = x$ gives pop quizzes, $Ex = x$ excuses students who cut on days when pop quizzes are given, $Px = x$ penalizes those students who attend class)

218. Any conservative who supports legislation which bans communist speakers from campus is inconsistent. Proof: A conservative who supports legislation which unnecessarily curtails freedom is inconsistent. Any person who backs legislation prohibiting communists from speaking on campus is supporting legislation which unnecessarily restricts our freedom.

(Universe of discourse: persons; $Ax = x$ is a conservative, $Bx = x$ supports communist-speaker-ban legislation, $Dx = x$ is consistent, $Ex = x$ supports legislation which unnecessarily curtails freedom)

219. The philosopher Antony Flew has argued that religious utterances (for example, 'God is love') are, strictly speaking, meaningless.[93] The bones of his reasoning are represented by 219.

> All meaningful nonanalytic statements are (in principle) falsifiable. Religious statements are neither analytic nor (in principle) falsifiable. Hence religious statements aren't meaningful.

(Universe of discourse: statements; $Mx = x$ is meaningful, $Ax = x$ is analytic, $Fx = x$ is (in principle) falsifiable, $Rx = x$ is religious)

220. The philosopher of religion John Hick disagrees with the first premise and the conclusion of the preceding argument.[94] His criticism of the premise runs on the order of 220.

> Any statement which is (in principle) verifiable is meaningful. The sentence 'Somewhere there is a stone which weighs more than five pounds' is (a) nonanalytic, (b) (in principle) verifiable, and (c) not (even in principle) falsifiable. So it is false that all meaningful nonanalytic statements are (in principle) falsifiable.

(Universe of discourse: statements; $Vx = x$ is verifiable, $Mx, s =$ the sentence 'Somewhere there is a stone which weighs more than five pounds,' $Ax = x$ is analytic, $Fx = x$ is falsifiable)

221. Hick rejects the conclusion of 219 and maintains that at least some religious statements (for example 'God exists') are meaningful. Argument 221 summarizes his reasoning.

---

[93] See Flew's "Theology and Falsification," in *New Essays in Philosophical Theology*, ed. by Antony Flew and Alasdair MacIntyre.
[94] See Hick, "Theology and Verification," *Theology Today*, XVII (1960), 12–31.

We can make sense of the notion of being resurrected in another realm and of having experiences in such a realm which would provide evidence for the existence of God. (W) If this is so, then the sentence 'God exists' is (in principle) verifiable. But any statement which is (in principle) verifiable is meaningful. Hence the sentence 'God exists' is meaningful.

(Universe of discourse: statements; $W, s =$ the sentence 'God exists,' Vx, Mx)

222. The Chinese philosopher Chuang Tzu held that philosophical disputes can't be satisfactorily settled—even with the services of an arbitrator.[95] He reasoned:

An arbitrator who agrees with (at least) one party to the dispute will be useless. But an arbitrator who agrees with no party to the dispute will also be useless. So arbitrators are not useful.

($Ax = x$ is an arbitrator, $Bx = x$ agrees with (at least) one party to the dispute, $Ux = x$ is useless)

223. In the *Leviathan*,[96] Thomas Hobbes reasons:

Understanding involves language. Therefore if only men use language, then only men understand.

($Ux = x$ understands, $Lx = x$ uses language, $Mx = x$ is a man)

224.   If God does not exist, then there will be no heaven and no hell. If he does exist, then the only human suffering that exists is such as to somehow help in the fulfilling of God's purpose. Eternal

---

[95] See Waley, *Three Ways of Thought in Ancient China*, p. 10.
[96] P. 38.

human suffering could not help fulfill God's purpose. But there will be unending human suffering if there is a hell. It follows that hell does not exist. (B)

($G =$ God exists, $A =$ Heaven exists, B, $Sx = x$ is human suffering, $Px = x$ helps fulfill God's purpose, $Ux = x$ is unending)

225. No syllogism which has two particular premises is valid.[97] This can be proved by an extended chain of reasoning represented by arguments 225 through 229.

Any syllogism with two "I" premises commits the fallacy of undistributed middle and any syllogism with two "O" premises commits the fallacy of negative premises. No valid syllogism commits either of these fallacies. Hence any syllogism which has either two "I" premises or two "O" premises is invalid.

(Universe of discourse: syllogisms; $Ix = x$ has two "I" premises, $Ux = x$ commits the fallacy of undistributed middle, $Ox = x$ has two "O" premises, $Nx = x$ commits the fallacy of negative premises, Vx)

226.   Any syllogism with an "O" premise and an affirmative conclusion commits the "negative premise—affirmative conclusion" fallacy. No valid syllogism commits this fallacy. A syllogism has a negative conclusion if and only if it does not have an affirmative one. It follows that any valid syllogism with an "O" premise has a negative conclusion.

(Universe of discourse: syllogisms; $Ox = x$ has an "O" premise, $Ax = x$ has an affirmative conclusion, $Fx = x$ commits the "negative

[97] Actually there are exceptions to this generalization, but because of their rarity most logic texts overlook them. Each of the arguments from 225 through 229 contains one or more premises to which there are exceptions.

premise—affirmative conclusion" fallacy, $Vx, Nx = x$ has a negative conclusion)

227.   Any valid syllogism with an "O" premise has a negative conclusion. Every syllogism with a negative conclusion distributes the major term in the conclusion. All syllogisms which distribute the major term in the conclusion but not in the major premise commit the fallacy of illicit process of the major. Only invalid syllogisms commit this fallacy. Therefore any valid syllogism with an "O" premise distributes the major term in the major premise.

(Universe of discourse: syllogisms; $Vx, Ox, Nx, Cx = x$ distributes the major term in its conclusion, $Px = x$ distributes the major term in its major premise, $Fx = x$ commits the fallacy of illicit process of the major)

228.   Any valid syllogism with an "O" premise distributes the major term in the major premise. Every valid syllogism distributes the middle term at least once. Any syllogism which distributes the major term in its major premise and the middle term at least once has at least two distributed terms in its premises. No syllogism with an "I" premise and an "O" premise has at least two distributed terms in its premises. Thus no syllogism with an "I" premise and an "O" premise is valid.

(Universe of discourse: syllogisms; $Vx, Ox, Px, Mx = x$ distributes the middle term at least once, $Tx = x$ has at least two distributed terms in its premises, $Ix = x$ has an "I" premise)

229. This concludes the chain of reasoning which started with 225.

        (As 226 through 228 established) no syllogism with an "I" premise and an "O" premise is valid. (As 225 proved) every syllogism which has either two "I" premises or two "O" premises is invalid. If a syllogism has two particular premises, it either has an "I" and an "O" premise or it has two "I"s or it has two "O"s. Hence no syllogism with two particular premises is valid.

(Universe of discourse: syllogisms; $Ax = x$ has an "I" premise and an "O" premise, Vx, $Ix = x$ has two "I" premises, $Ox = x$ has two "O" premises, $Px = x$ has two particular premises)

230. The philosopher and mathematician Frege believed that there exists, in addition to the physical and mental realms, a third realm which contains propositions.[98] One of his arguments for this view is paraphrased by 230.

> There are propositions. They are sharable, but not perceivable by the senses. Nothing in the mental realm is sharable. Everything in the physical realm is perceivable by the senses. Therefore there exist entities belonging neither to the physical realm nor to the mental realm.

($Ax = x$ is a proposition, $Bx = x$ is sharable, $Cx = x$ is perceivable by the senses, $Mx = x$ is mental, $Px = x$ is physical)

231.   All my philosophy books are in the office, except for the ones I have lent. Every book that I have lent is noted on this list. *The Concept of Mind* is one of my philosophy books which is not noted on the list. So it must be in my office.

(Universe of discourse: my books; $Px = x$ is on the subject of philosophy, $Ox = x$ is in my office, $Lx = $ I have lent x, $Nx = x$ is noted on this list, $c = $ *The Concept of Mind*)

---

[98] See Gottlob Frege, "The Thought: A Logical Inquiry," trans. by A. M. and Marcelle Quinton, *Mind*, LXV (1956), 289–311.

232. The nature of mathematics has been a matter for philosophical dispute for centuries. Arguments 232 through 234 give the briefest of outlines for three views advanced on this subject by (among others) John Stuart Mill, A. J. Ayer, and Immanuel Kant. Argument 232 reflects Mill's position:[99]

> Mathematical propositions have content. Only synthetic propositions have content. There aren't any synthetic a priori propositions.[100] Every proposition is either a priori or a posteriori. It follows that mathematical propositions are synthetic a posteriori.

(Universe of discourse: propositions; $Mx = x$ is mathematical, $Cx = x$ has content, $Sx = x$ is synthetic, $Bx = x$ is a priori, $Dx = x$ is a posteriori)

233.   Mathematical propositions are necessary. A posteriori propositions are not necessary. There aren't any synthetic a priori propositions. Every proposition is either synthetic or analytic, and either a priori or a posteriori. So mathematical propositions are analytic a priori.[101]

---

[99] See Mill's A System of Logic, Rationative and Inductive, Bk. II, chs. 5–7.

[100] This premise is a cardinal principle of empiricism. It is accepted by Ayer, also, but is rejected by Kant. Rough definitions for the four technical terms employed in 232 through 234:

> analytic means true (or false) by virtue of the meanings of terms;
> synthetic means not analytic;
> a priori means independent of experience;
> a posteriori means dependent on experience.

For more adequate definitions of these four terms and a discussion of the nature of mathematics, see Stephen F. Barker, Philosophy of Mathematics.

[101] See Ayer, Language, Truth and Logic, ch. 4.

(Universe of discourse: propositions; see 232 for the meanings of some of the following; Mx, $Nx = x$ is necessary, Dx, Sx, Bx, $Ax = x$ is analytic)

234. Mathematical propositions are necessary. Only a priori propositions are necessary. Mathematical propositions have content. Only synthetic propositions have content. Therefore mathematical propositions are synthetic a priori.[102]

(Universe of discourse: propositions; see 232 and 233 for symbols)

235. The most famous argument *against* the existence of God is the argument from evil, which can be formulated:

> If there is a perfect being, he is omniscient, omnipotent, and all good. If there is an omniscient, omnipotent, and all good being, then there will be no natural catastrophes. Since natural catastrophes do occur, there must not be a perfect being.

($Px = x$ is perfect, $Yx = x$ is omniscient, $Zx = x$ is omnipotent, $Ax = x$ is all good, $Nx = x$ is a natural catastrophe)

236. A conditional is a sentence of the form "If p, then q." By definition, a *truth-functional* conditional is one which is false if and only if its antecedent (the "p" part) is true and its consequent (the "q" part) false. Argument 236 proves that not all conditionals are truth-functional.

> A truth-functional conditional is false if and only if its antecedent is true and its consequent false. The sentence 'If Columbus

---

[102] See Kant, *Critique of Pure Reason*, pp. 52–53.

had died at age ten, then no Europeans would ever have reached America' is false; yet it does not have a true antecedent. This is proof that some conditionals aren't truth-functional.

(Universe of discourse: conditional sentences; $Tx = x$ is truth-functional, $Fx = x$ is false, $Ax = x$ has a true antecedent, $Cx = x$ has a false consequent, $s =$ the sentence 'If Columbus had died at age ten, then no Europeans would ever have reached America')

237. In *The Principles of Human Knowledge,* Berkeley advances many arguments against the belief that there are material objects. In one he maintains that everything can be explained without assuming the existence of material bodies. He concludes as follows:

> If therefore it were possible for bodies to exist without [that is, outside of] the mind, yet to hold that they do so must needs be a very precarious opinion, since it is to suppose, without any reason at all, that God has created innumerable beings that are entirely useless and serve to no manner of purpose.[103]

This argument can easily be formalized:

If material objects exist, they have no use. God would not create anything which is entirely useless. If there are material objects, they were created by God. Therefore there are no material objects.

($Mx = x$ is a material object, $Ux = x$ is useless, $Gx = x$ is created by God)

---

[103] P. 32.

238. Another Berkeleyan argument[104] against the belief in material objects:

> Anything which can be known at all can be known either by sense or by reason. Anything which can be known by sense is a sensation. If there are material objects existing outside the mind, they are not sensations. It is possible that we could have sensations even though there were no material objects. (P) If this is so, then there is no necessary connection between material objects and sensations. But if there is no necessary connection between material objects and sensations, then if there are material objects existing outside the mind, they can't be known by reason. Hence if there are material objects existing outside the mind, they cannot be known.

($Kx = x$ can be known, $Sx = x$ can be known by sense, $Rx = x$ can be known by reason, $Ax = x$ is a sensation, $Mx = x$ is a material object existing outside the mind, P, $N =$ There is a necessary connection between material objects and sensations)

239. Naturally Berkeley is critical of the view that our sensations resemble material objects (the view of *representative perception*). Argument 239 contains one of his attacks on this doctrine.[105] (See 301 for another criticism by Berkeley.)

> If those things which our sensations (supposedly) resemble are perceivable, then they are ideas. If, on the other hand, they are not perceivable, then our sensations cannot resemble them. Thus if our sensations resemble anything they resemble ideas.

($Rx = x$ is resembled by a sensation, $Px = x$ is perceivable, $Ix = x$ is an idea)

---

[104] *Ibid.*, pp. 31–32.
[105] *Ibid.*, pp. 26–27.

240. This argument establishes a logical principle which is employed in connection with 111, 129, 174, 268, and 320.

If the premise set of an argument is not contradictory but its conclusion *is* contradictory, then it is logically possible that all of its premises are true and its conclusion false. No argument for which this is a logical possibility is valid. Hence any valid argument which has a contradictory conclusion also has a contradictory premise set.

(Universe of discourse: arguments; $Px = x$ has a contradictory premise set, $Cx = x$ has a contradictory conclusion, $Lx =$ it is logically possible that the premises of x are true and the conclusion of x false, Vx)

241.   No perfect being is immoral. Any individual who fails to value intellectual honesty is imperfect. No moral individual who values intellectual honesty would punish agnosticism. Therefore if God is perfect he will not punish agnosticism.

(Universe of discourse: beings; $Px = x$ is perfect, $Mx = x$ is moral, $Vx = x$ values intellectual honesty, $Ax = x$ punishes agnosticism, $g =$ God)

242. Commentators on Wittgenstein's *Tractatus* disagree about whether he regarded properties as objects. George Pitcher[106] supports his view on the issue with this argument.

Properties are either formal or material. Objects can be represented. Formal properties cannot be. Material properties are produced by the configuration of objects. No objects can be produced by the configuration of objects. Consequently no properties are objects.

---

[106] *The Philosophy of Wittgenstein,* p. 115. Irving Copi devised the argument.

Pitcher claims that the premises of this argument are all Wittgensteinian theses, and reasons that if Wittgenstein was logically consistent he accepted the conclusion. ($Px = x$ is a property, $Fx = x$ is a formal property, $Mx = x$ is a material property, $Ox = x$ is an object, $Rx = x$ can be represented, $Cx = x$ is produced by the configuration of objects)

243. Some people maintain that causality is a relationship of "entailment." [107] Argument 243 criticizes this view.

> 'A entails B' means it is not logically possible that A is true and B false. (M). If this is correct, then only truth-value bearers (that is, things which are true or false) can enter into entailment relations. It makes no sense to speak of events as being true or false. (S) If this doesn't make sense, then events don't bear truth values. Causality is a relationship between events. (Y) If it is and if no events enter into relationships of entailment, then causality is not an entailment relationship. We conclude that causality is not a relationship of entailment. (Z)

($M = $ 'A entails B' means it is not logically possible that A is true and B false, $Tx = x$ is a truth-value bearer, $Rx = x$ enters into entailment relations, $S = $ It makes sense to speak of events as being true or false, $Ex = x$ is an event, Y, Z)

244.   If everything is regarded as clear, then nothing needs explanation. If nothing is regarded as clear, then nothing can be explained. So if something both needs to be, and can be, explained, then some things are taken to be clear and some things are not taken to be clear.[108]

---

[107] A. C. Ewing advances this view in chapter eight of *The Fundamental Questions of Philosophy*.
[108] See Nelson Goodman, *Fact, Fiction, and Forecast*, p. 31.

(Universe of discourse: objects of understanding; $Cx = x$ is regarded as clear, $Ax = x$ needs explanation, $Bx = x$ can be explained)

245.   Anyone who believes that we have sound evidence for the harmfulness of smoking but who publicly denies this is immoral. Any tobacco industry spokesman who does not believe that we have gathered sound evidence that smoking is harmful is basing his beliefs on his hopes. It follows that any spokesman for the tobacco industry who publicly denies that we have sound evidence for the harmfulness of smoking is either immoral or is founding his beliefs on hopes.

(Universe of discourse: persons; $Bx = x$ believes that we have sound evidence for the harmfulness of smoking, $Dx = x$ publicly denies that we have sound evidence for the harmfulness of smoking, $Ix = x$ is immoral, $Tx = x$ is a tobacco industry spokesman, $Hx = x$ bases his beliefs on his hopes)

246.   If no one contributes to CARE, then someone perishes from hunger. Therefore there is a person who perishes from hunger if he doesn't contribute to CARE.

It seems obvious that 246 is invalid. Nevertheless, when it is symbolized in the standard fashion, the symbolization is found valid. On first glance this appears to reveal a defect in the present state of symbolic logic.[109] Prove that the symbolized version of 246 is valid. (Universe of discourse: persons; $Cx = x$ contributes to CARE, $Px = x$ perishes from hunger)

---

[109] A second problematic example:

> There is a garbage collector who does not enter the presidential race. So there is a garbage collector who wins the presidential race if he enters it.

The ordinary symbolization of this argument is valid, yet the English argument seems invalid.

247.   The Salem authorities spared a person accused of witch-craft if and only if he "confessed" to being a witch. All the accused who "confessed" to being witches when they were not actually witches perjured themselves. Only those accused who "confessed" to being witches perjured themselves. Of course, none of the accused actually was a witch. This means that the authorities spared all the accused who perjured themselves and only those accused who perjured themselves.

(Universe of discourse: Salemites accused of witchcraft; $Sx = x$ was spared by the authorities, $Cx = x$ "confessed" to being a witch, $Wx = x$ was a witch, $Px = x$ perjured himself)

248.   A syllogism which has a universal conclusion distributes the minor term in the conclusion. A valid syllogism which distributes the minor term in the conclusion distributes that term in its premise set.[110] Every valid syllogism has at least one distributed middle term. If a syllogism distributes its middle term at least once and also distributes the minor term in its premise set, it will have more than one term distributed in its premise set. All valid syllogisms which have affirmative conclusions have two affirmative premises. No syllogism with two affirmative premises and a particular premise will have more than one term distributed in the premise set. It follows from the above that no valid syllogism with a universal affirmative conclusion will have a particular premise.

(Universe of discourse: syllogisms; $Ax = x$ has a universal conclusion, $Bx = x$ distributes the minor term in the conclusion, Vx, $Cx = x$ distributes the minor term in its premise set, $Dx = x$ has at least one distributed middle term, $Ex = x$ has more than one term distributed in its premise set, $Fx = x$ has an affirmative conclusion, $Gx = x$ has two affirmative premises, $Hx = x$ has a particular premise)

---

[110] There are rare exceptions to this generalization, and to other generalizations in 248 through 250.

249.   Any syllogism with a universal negative conclusion distributes both the minor term and the major term in the conclusion. A syllogism which distributes both the minor and major terms in the conclusion is valid only if it distributes both those terms in the premise set. Any valid syllogism has at least one distributed middle term. Any syllogism which distributes both the major and minor terms in its premise set and in addition has at least one distributed middle term will distribute more than two terms in its premise set. Every valid syllogism has at least one affirmative premise. No syllogism which has a particular premise and at least one affirmative premise will have more than two terms distributed in its premise set. Therefore no valid syllogism with a universal negative conclusion will have a particular premise.

(Universe of discourse: syllogisms; see 248 for the meanings of some of the symbols; Ax, $Ix = x$ has a negative conclusion, $Jx = x$ distributes both the minor and the major terms in the conclusion, Vx, $Kx = x$ distributes both the minor and the major terms in its premise set, Dx, $Lx = x$ has more than two terms distributed in its premise set, $Mx = x$ has at least one affirmative premise, Hx)

250.   (Argument 248 shows that) no valid syllogism with a universal *affirmative* conclusion will have a particular premise. (Argument 249 shows that) no valid syllogism with a universal *negative* conclusion will have a particular premise. Any syllogism which has a universal conclusion will have either an affirmative or a negative conclusion. A syllogism has a particular conclusion if and only if it does not have a universal conclusion. Hence any valid syllogism with a particular premise has a particular conclusion.

(Universe of discourse: syllogisms; see 248 for the meanings of some of the symbols; Vx, Ax, Fx, Hx, $Ix = x$ has a negative conclusion, $Nx = x$ has a particular conclusion)

5 | Valid and Invalid Nonrelational Quantificational Arguments

251. Every analytic statement is a priori. This proves that a statement is a priori if and only if it is analytic, since none but a priori statements are analytic.

(Universe of discourse: statements; $Bx = x$ is analytic, $Cx = x$ is a priori)

252. The philosopher William Alston notes that although arguments 252 and 253 look very much alike, they are quite different logically.[111] He concludes from this that sentences which have proper names for subjects are of a different logical form from sentences which have the word 'someone' as subject.

Joe Carpenter sells insurance in our town. Joe Carpenter belongs to the First Methodist Church. Therefore, Joe Carpenter both sells insurance in our town and belongs to the First Methodist Church.

---

[111] See *Philosophy of Language*, pp. 3–4.

(j = Joe Carpenter, $Ix = x$ sells insurance in our town, $Mx = x$ belongs to the First Methodist Church)

253.   Someone sells insurance in our town. Someone belongs to the First Methodist Church. Therefore, someone both sells insurance in our town and belongs to the First Methodist Church.

(Ix, Mx)

254.   When insurance comes to you with imagination it comes to you from INA. So all INA insurance comes to you with imagination.

($Ax = x$ is insurance which comes to you with imagination, $Bx = x$ is INA insurance)

255. This exchange took place in the philosophy office:

> Nosy secretary: "Did the Schippers invite all the faculty members?"
> Pospesel: "No, they didn't invite me."

I am making a simple inference which is formalized:

The Schippers did not invite Pospesel. Pospesel is a faculty member. Hence it is false that the Schippers invited all the faculty members.

($Sx = x$ was invited by the Schippers, p = Pospesel, $Fx = x$ is a faculty member)

256. A tire commercial proclaims "If it doesn't say 'Goodyear,' then it can't be Polyglas." Does this entail that all Polyglas tires say

"Goodyear"? (Universe of discourse: tires; $Gx = x$ says "Goodyear," $Px = x$ is Polyglas)

257.   Any argument which is not truth-functionally valid is not valid. This follows from the fact that every truth-functionally valid argument is valid.

(Universe of discourse: arguments; $Tx = x$ is truth-functionally valid, $Vx = x$ is valid)

258.   All Lutherans are Protestants. Therefore some Lutherans are Protestants.

This argument is discussed in 161 and 162. (Lx, Px)

259. Analyze 258 using "Lutherans" as the universe of discourse. If you get discrepant results, can you account for them? (Px)

260. Add 'There are Lutherans' to the premise set of 258, and re-evaluate the argument. (Lx, Px)

261. An editorial in *The Miami News* charged that only the children of influential people were enrolled in the University of Miami's laboratory school. A parent replied to this charge in a letter to the editor.[112] Argument 261 reproduces her reasoning.

      Certainly University President Stanford has influence; yet he was unable to enroll his child in West Lab. Therefore it is false that only persons with influence get their children enrolled.

---

[112] See "A Parent Defends West Lab School," *The Miami News,* January 24, 1969, p. 12–A.

(s = President Stanford, $Ix = x$ has influence, $Ex =$ a child of x is enrolled in West Lab)

262. Many people (especially authors of high-school English texts) maintain that a valid deductive argument is one which proceeds from the general to the specific and that a correct inductive argument proceeds from the specific to the general.[113] Let's concentrate on the first half of this claim (the part dealing with deduction). Arguments 262 through 264 do not proceed from the general to the specific. So if any one of them is deductively valid, the above-mentioned claim is mistaken. Argument 262 is an example of passing from general to general.

> All cats are mammals. Hence all cats are either mammals or reptiles.

(Cx, Mx, Rx)

263. This argument is an example of passing from specific to specific.

> Jones is a tall alcoholic. So Jones is tall.

(j, Tx, Ax)

264. This argument passes from specific to general.

> Brown is a Republican labor leader. It follows that some labor leaders are Republicans.

(b, Rx, Lx)

---

[113] For a refutation of both parts of this claim see Brian Skyrms, *Choice and Chance: An Introduction to Inductive Logic,* pp. 13–15.

265.   There are valid deductive arguments which do not proceed from the general to the specific. So it is false that all valid deductive arguments proceed from the general to the specific.

(Universe of discourse: valid deductive arguments; $Px = x$ proceeds from the general to the specific)

266. An advertisement posted on collegiate bulletin boards reads "Jaguar by Yardley has insured you for $10,000 (in case you're maimed, mauled, trampled and dismembered by 50 or more frenzied females)." Sophomore Gerald Swindle conceived the idea of paying the girls of Pi Upsilon $2,000 to maul and trample him in a frenzied manner. However, he gave the idea up—partly as a result of his logical researches. Obviously he was toying with argument 266.

Anyone maimed, mauled, trampled and dismembered by 50 or more frenzied females is eligible to collect $10,000 from Yardley. Gerald Swindle was mauled and trampled by 50 or more frenzied females. Therefore he is eligible to collect $10,000 from Yardley.

($Yx = x$ is maimed by 50 or more frenzied females, $Zx = x$ is mauled by . . . females, $Tx = x$ is trampled by . . . females, $Dx = x$ is dismembered by . . . females, $Ex = x$ is eligible to collect $10,000 from Yardley, s = Gerald Swindle)

267. The sentence 'All cats are dogs' is obviously false—but is it necessarily false or empirically false? As a means to obtaining the answer determine whether it is entailed by the empirically false sentence 'There are no cats.' If determining whether this entailment holds does not give you the answer about the status of 'All cats are dogs,' cheat and look at argument 294. (Cx, Dx)

268. Pondering on the preceding example might lead one to believe that no sentence of the form 'All A are B' could be necessarily false. But what of this sentence?

All things which are either cats or noncats are both dogs and nondogs.

Is this necessarily false? Find out by determining whether it entails the necessarily false sentence 'Everything is both a cat and a noncat.' (Cx, Dx)

269. Descartes thought the human soul was connected to the body at the *pineal gland*. One could argue for this thesis with 269. (The third premise was accepted by Descartes, although it is now known to be false.)

There is an organ in the human body where the soul joins the body. Any organ where the human body and the soul are joined must be one which animals lack. Animals do not possess the pineal gland. Consequently the pineal gland is an organ in the human body where the soul and body intersect.

$(Ox = x$ is an organ in the human body where the soul joins the body, $Ax = x$ is an organ which animals possess, $p =$ the pineal gland)

270. The logicians Terrell and Baker include a symbolized version of 270 in a set of (purportedly) valid arguments.[114] Does it belong there?

---

[114] See D. B. Terrell and Robert Baker, *Exercises in Logic*, p. 177, problem 2. Also cf. problems 3 and 4 on p. 175.

If either everything is C or everything is M, then nothing is D. Some things are both D and E. Therefore something is neither C nor M.

(Cx, Mx, Dx, Ex)

271. We were discussing the concept of "event" in an introductory philosophy class, and considering the question whether *thinking about a girlfriend* should be counted as an event. A student who thought it should advanced 271 (using some of my remarks for his first two premises).

Every event occurs in time. Nothing which has weight is an event. Thinking about your girlfriend occurs in time but lacks weight. Hence thinking about a girlfriend is an event.

$(Ex = x$ is an event, $Tx = x$ occurs in time, $Wx = x$ has weight, $Gx = x$ is an instance of thinking about a girlfriend)

272. Is the truth of the premises of a valid deductive argument a necessary condition for the truth of the conclusion? Argument 272 purports to prove the negative answer to this question.

Some deductive arguments which have true conclusions but not true premises are valid.[115] Thus it is not the case that the truth of the premises of a valid deductive argument is a necessary condition for the truth of the conclusion.

(Universe of discourse: deductive arguments; $Cx = x$ has a true conclusion, $Px = x$ has true premises, Vx)

273.   Some philosophical propositions are (1) meaningful, (2)

---

[115] E.g.: Everything is red; therefore something is red.

nonempirical, and (3) not without content. All analytic propositions are contentless. Therefore the thesis that meaningful propositions divide up into the exclusive and exhaustive camps of *analytic* and *empirical* is false.

(Universe of discourse: propositions; $Px = x$ is philosophical, $Mx = x$ is meaningful, $Ex = x$ is empirical, $Cx = x$ has content, $Ax = x$ is analytic)

274. In the *Leviathan,* Hobbes writes:

> . . . *True* and *false* are attributes of speech, not of things. And where speech is not, there is neither *truth* nor *falsehood.*[116]

How are these two assertions related logically (that is, does either entail the other)? Find out by evaluating arguments 274 and 275.

> *True* and *false* are attributes of speech only. So if there is no speech, then there is neither truth nor falsehood.

($Tx = x$ is true, $Fx = x$ is false, $Sx = x$ is speech)

275.   If there is no speech, then there is neither truth nor falsehood. So *true* and *false* are attributes of speech only.

(See 274.)

276. In "The Theory of Meaning," Gilbert Ryle writes:

> Proper names are appellations and not descriptions; and descriptions are descriptions and not appellations.[117]

[116] P. 34.
[117] P. 248.

Does the clause preceding the semicolon entail the clause which follows the semicolon? ($Px = x$ is a proper name, $Ax = x$ is an appellation, $Dx = x$ is a description)

277. Argument 20 is an unsuccessful attack on a claim made by Bertrand Russell. A second attempt follows:

> There are philosophical inferences not belonging to logic which are important even though not inductive. All philosophical inferences are outside the areas of mathematics, law, and theology. This establishes the falsity of the claim that all important inferences outside of logic, mathematics, law, and theology are inductive.

(Universe of discourse: inferences; $Px = x$ belongs to philosophy, $Lx = x$ belongs to logic, $Ax = x$ is important, $Bx = x$ is inductive, $Cx = x$ belongs to mathematics, law, or theology)

278. In *Language, Truth and Logic,* [118] A. J. Ayer reasons:

> If empiricism is correct, then no proposition which has factual content can be necessary. Accordingly if empiricism is correct, then either all mathematical propositions lack necessity or they all lack factual content.

(E = Empiricism is correct, $Fx = x$ is a factual proposition, $Nx = x$ is a necessary proposition, $Mx = x$ is a mathematical proposition)

279. Use care in symbolizing this argument.

> Only doctors and hospital administrators are eligible. Mrs.

---

[118] Pp. 72–73.

Schuh is eligible. Therefore Mrs. Schuh is a doctor and a hospital administrator.

$(Dx, Hx, Ex, s = \text{Mrs. Schuh})$

280. Replace the conclusion of 278 with the logically weaker statement 'Therefore if empiricism is correct, then any mathematical proposition lacks either necessity or factual content.' Reassess the argument. (See 278.)

281. Strengthen the premise set of 278 by adding to it 'Either all mathematical propositions are necessary or all are factual.' Evaluate the resulting argument. (See 278.)

282.   Either all of the houses being built across the street are going to be sales models or none will be models. Some of those houses are being built under FHA. No models are built under FHA. So none of the houses going up across the street will be models.

$(Hx = x$ is a house being built across the street, $Mx = x$ will be a model, $Fx = x$ is being built under FHA$)$

283. Argument 10 attacked the "name" theory of meaning. Another criticism of this view is provided by 283.[119]

If every word is a name, then every sentence which contains more than one word is a list. Lists do not have truth values. Some sentences do have truth values. It follows that some words are not names.

---

[119] This argument is based on a discussion by Ryle in "The Theory of Meaning," p. 244. See also 176 and 321.

($Wx = x$ is a word, $Nx = x$ is a name, $Sx = x$ is a sentence, $Cx = x$ contains more than one word, $Lx = x$ is a list, $Tx = x$ has a truth value)

284. An attempted improvement on 59:

> Every false sentence either (1) asserts what isn't the case or (2) denies what is the case. Any sentence which does the former is one which maintains that something is the case, and any sentence which does the latter is one which denies that something is the case. Now no sentence which either asserts or denies something to be the case is meaningless. Hence no sentence is both false and meaningless.

(Universe of discourse: sentences; Fx, $Yx = x$ asserts what isn't the case, $Zx = x$ denies what is the case, $Ax = x$ asserts that something is the case, $Dx = x$ denies that something is the case, $Mx = x$ is meaningless)

285. Add the obvious truth 'Some sentences contain more than one word' to the premise set of 283 and reevaluate it. (See 283.)

286. Mrs. Shick was not much good at kitten sexing, but she could reason:

> All of Smudgie's kittens look alike in the relevant respects. (L) If so, then either all of them are males or all are females. Some of the kittens are calicoes. All calicoes are females. Therefore all of Smudgie's kittens are females.

(Universe of discourse: Smudgie's kittens; L, $Mx = x$ is male, $Fx = x$ is female, $Cx = x$ is calico)

287. Substitute 'Some sentences of more than one word have truth values' for the third premise of 283. Is the resulting argument valid? (See 283.)

288. Add to the premise set of 286 the following:

> None of Smudgie's kittens is both male and female.

Evaluate the revised argument. (See 286.)

289. When 56 is strengthened by the addition of these two premises, is the resulting argument valid? [120]

> There are laws of physics. Either all propositions are mind-dependent or else none are.

($Lx = x$ is a law of physics, $Px = x$ is a proposition, $Hx = x$ will hold when all human minds have disappeared, $Mx = x$ is mind-dependent)

290. (DIFFICULT)

> Whatever exists is material. Hence exactly one of the following two claims is true: (1) nothing is mental; (2) some material things are mental, and all mental things are material.

($Ax = x$ is material, $Bx = x$ is mental)

---

[120] Argument 289 paraphrases reasoning presented by Fitch in "The Reality of Propositions," p. 7.

6 | Valid Relational Arguments

291.   Sam loves everybody. So Sam loves himself.

(Universe of discourse: persons; $s = $ Sam, $Lxy = x$ loves y[121])

292.   There is no number which is larger than all numbers. This is a consequence of the fact that no number is larger than itself.

(Universe of discourse: numbers; $Lxy = x$ is larger than y)

293.   God was not created by anything. Therefore it is false that God created everything.

($g = $ God, $Cxy = x$ created y)

294. This argument relates to exercise 267:

---

[121] Following 'L' with 'xy' indicates that 'L' is a *two-place relation* symbol. In symbolizing sentences you may choose other *individual* symbols. For example, in a given case you may wish to follow 'L' with 'yx,' 'zz,' or 'ab.'

Only necessarily false statements entail necessary falsities. The sentence 'There are no cats' is not necessarily false, but it entails 'All cats are dogs.' So 'All cats are dogs' is not necessarily false.

(Universe of discourse: statements; $Nx = x$ is necessarily false, $Exy = x$ entails y, $t =$ the sentence 'There are no cats,' $a =$ the sentence 'All cats are dogs')

295. Nelson Goodman considers and rejects this definition of 'representation' (in art):[122]

A represents B if and only if A resembles B.

His criticism of the definition:

Everything resembles itself. Something does not represent itself. Hence it is false that one thing represents another if and only if it resembles the other.

($Cxy = x$ resembles y, $Dxy = x$ represents y)

296.   "Entailment" is a *transitive* relation.[123] So if one statement entails a second but does not entail a third, then the second statement also does not entail the third.

(Universe of discourse: statements; Exy)

---

[122] See his *Languages of Art*, pp. 3–4.
[123] In other words, if one statement entails a second and the second statement entails a third, then the first entails the third. See 372.

297. William James's principal argument for indeterminism may be paraphrased in this way:[124]

> Indeterminism satisfies human needs more adequately than does determinism. Of two conceptions, the one which more adequately satisfies human needs is the more rational. Of two conceptions, we are entitled to suppose that the more rational is the truer. Thus we are entitled to suppose indeterminism to be truer than determinism.

(Universe of discourse: conceptions; i = indeterminism, $Sxy = x$ satisfies human needs more adequately than y, d = determinism, $Rxy = x$ is more rational than y, Txy = we are entitled to suppose x to be truer than y)

298.   Mental events are not located anywhere. Hence they are not located in brains.

($Mx = x$ is a mental event, $Lxy = x$ is located in y, $Bx = x$ is a brain)

299.   For every proposition there is at least one proposition which entails it and at least one proposition which it entails. This follows from the fact that every proposition entails itself.

(Universe of discourse: propositions; $Exy = x$ entails y)

300. Dave's Shell Station advertises in the *Miami Hurricane* that it "specializes in the repair of all American and foreign cars." Argument 300 convicts Dave of misusing the concept "specialize."

---

[124] James argues for the first and third premises in "The Dilemma of Determinism," and for the second premise in "The Sentiment of Rationality," in *Essays in Pragmatism*, ed. by Alburey Castell.

(Because of the meaning of the word 'specialize') no garage specializes in the repair of *all* cars. Dave's Shell Station is a garage. Any car is either American or foreign. This shows it is false that Dave's Shell Station specializes in the repair of all American and foreign cars.

($Gx = x$ is a garage, $Sxy = x$ specializes in the repair of y, $Cx = x$ is a car, $d =$ Dave's Shell Station, $Ax = x$ is American, $Fx = x$ is foreign)

301. The doctrine of *representative perception* maintains that our sensations are caused by material objects and that the sensations represent or picture these objects. Berkeley attacked this doctrine with several arguments, including 301.[125]

Our sensations are not causes. Anything which represents or pictures something which is a cause must itself be a cause. So it is false that there are sensations which represent things which are causes.

($Sx = x$ is a sensation, $Cx = x$ is a cause, $Rxy = x$ represents or pictures y)

302. Tobacco companies actually favor the warnings which they are required to print on cigarette packages, because these warnings reduce their liability in damage suits brought against them by ill ex-smokers and the warnings accomplish this without decreasing the sales of cigarettes. Obviously the tobacco companies favor anything which reduces liability without hurting cigarette sales.

---

[125] See *The Principles of Human Knowledge*, p. 35. Argument 239 is another attack.

($Tx = x$ is a tobacco company, $Fxy = x$ favors y, $Wx = x$ is a cigarette-package warning, $Rx = x$ reduces the liability of tobacco companies in damage suits, $Dx = x$ decreases cigarette sales)

303. Leibniz believed that there are no vacuums. Argument 303 is one of several arguments which he advanced in support of his belief.[126]

No possible world is better than our universe. Existence is better than nonexistence. (E) If this is so, then if two things are identical except that the first has matter where the second has a vacuum, then the first is better than the second. If our universe has a vacuum, then there is a possible world which is identical to it except that the possible world has matter where our actual universe has a vacuum. Therefore our universe does not contain a vacuum. (V)

($u =$ our universe, $Bxy = x$ is better than y, $Px = x$ is a possible world, E, $Ixy = x$ and y are identical except that x has matter where y has a vacuum, V)

304. Some logicians introduce a relation between statements which they label "material implication." One statement is said to materially imply a second if and only if the truth-functional conditional which has the first as antecedent and the second as consequent is true. One peculiarity of this relationship is that it is so often exemplified. As 304 shows, the relationship holds (in at least one direction) between any two statements.

All truth-functional conditionals with false antecedents are true. (A) If this is so, then a false statement materially implies all statements. All truth-functional conditionals with true consequents

---

[126] See *Leibniz Selections,* ed. by Philip P. Wiener, p. 236.

are true. (B) If this is correct, then a true statement is materially implied by all statements. Since every statement is either true or false, for any two statements either the first materially implies the second or the second materially implies the first or each materially implies the other.

(Universe of discourse: statements; A, $Fx = x$ is false, $Mxy = x$ materially implies y, B, $Tx = x$ is true)

305. The Aristotelian and Ptolemaic theory that the earth is the fixed center of the universe was supported by the following argument (among others).[127]

There is regularity in the heavens. (R) If so, then if one celestial body revolves around some object, then all the celestial bodies must revolve around that object. The moon is a celestial body which revolves around our earth. Therefore all celestial bodies revolve around the earth.

(R, $Cx = x$ is a celestial body, $Rxy = x$ revolves around y, $m =$ the moon, $e =$ the earth)

306. The main assumption of 305 was brought into question by Galileo's discovery of the satellites of Jupiter.[128]

There is at least one celestial body which revolves around Jupiter. The moon is a celestial body which does not revolve around Jupiter. So it is false that if one celestial body revolves around some object, then all the celestial bodies must revolve around that object.

(Cx, Rxy, $j =$ Jupiter, m)

---

[127] See Butterfield, *The Origins of Modern Science*, pp. 78–79.
[128] *Ibid.*, p. 79.

307.   This statement is false: a person can know something only
if it is *impossible* for him to be mistaken about it.[129] Its falsity
follows from two facts: (1) only logico-mathematical truths are
such that it is impossible for a person to be mistaken about them;
and (2) there are people who know something other than logico-
mathematical truths.

($Px = x$ is a person, $Kxy = x$ knows y, $Ixy =$ it is impossible for x
to be mistaken about y, $Lx = x$ is a logico-mathematical truth)

308. The statement whose falsity was demonstrated in 307 is frequently employed as a premise in arguments for skepticism.[130] Argument 308 is typical.

        A person can know something only if it is impossible for him
to be mistaken about it. Nothing relating to sense experience is
such that it is impossible for a person to be mistaken about it.
Accordingly no person knows anything which relates to sense
experience.

(See 307; Px, Kxy, Ixy, $Sx = x$ relates to sense experience)

309. Reasoning from premises which state that *each* individual member of some class has a certain property to the conclusion that *all*
members of that class have the property is called *complete induction*
(or *perfect induction*). (Complete "induction," in spite of the name,
is deductive.) Argument 309 is an example of this type of inference.

---

[129] It is important to distinguish this false claim from the true statement
'A person can know something only if he is not mistaken about it.'
[130] Cornman and Lehrer discuss this type of argument in chapter two of
Philosophical Problems and Arguments. Also cf. 37 in this volume.

Joe and Bob play the piano. Joe and Bob are the only Smith children.[131] Anything which is identical to a piano player is itself a piano player. Thus all of the Smith children play the piano.

(j = Joe, b = Bob, Px = x plays the piano, Sx = x is a Smith child, Ixy = x is identical to y)

310. The nineteenth-century logician Augustus De Morgan noted that traditional logic was unable to evaluate 310.

Horses are animals. Therefore heads of horses are heads of animals.

(Hx = x is a horse, Ax = x is an animal, Bxy = x is the head of y)

311. Since a tautology is without content it is plausible to assume that a tautology cannot contradict any statement. Such an assumption, however, is mistaken.[132]

Every tautology contradicts some statement. This is a consequence of three facts: (1) a logically false statement contradicts any statement; (2) there are logically false statements; and, (3) "contradiction" is a symmetrical relationship.[133]

---

131 In other words, Joe and Bob are Smith children and any Smith child is identical to either Joe or Bob.

132 'A contradicts B' is ambiguous; it may mean (1) "A and B are inconsistent" or (2) "A and B (logically) must have opposite truth values." The conclusion of 311 is true under either interpretation; however the first premise is true only if 'contradicts' has sense (1).

133 In other words, if one statement contradicts a second, then the second contradicts the first. See 386.

(Universe of discourse: statements; $Tx = x$ is a tautology, $Cxy = x$ contradicts y, $Fx = x$ is logically false)

312. It is commonly believed that if two sentences are logically equivalent, then they must also be synonymous. Sentences S1 and S2 constitute a counterexample:[134]

(S1) The winner was the tallest and James was the winner.
(S2) The winner was the tallest and James was the tallest.

Argument 312 formalizes the reasoning:

> Sentences S1 and S2 entail each other. Mutually entailing sentences are logically equivalent. A necessary condition for the synonymy of S1 and S2 is the synonymy of 'James was the winner' and 'James was the tallest.' These latter sentences, however, are not synonymous. "Synonymy" is a symmetrical relationship.[135] So the thesis that logically equivalent sentences are always synonymous is false.

(Universe of discourse: sentences; $a =$ sentence S1, $b =$ sentence S2, $Exy = x$ entails y, $Lxy = x$ is logically equivalent to y, $Sxy = x$ is synonymous with y, $w =$ the sentence 'James was the winner,' $t =$ the sentence 'James was the tallest')

313.   No university which operates on an inadequate budget should engage in any expensive programs which are not essen-

---

[134] This counterexample is provided by J. A. Faris in *Truth-Functional Logic*, p. 114. The following statements constitute a second counterexample:

Either it is raining or it is not raining.
Either it is cold or it is not cold.

[135] See 386.

tial either to academic excellence or to student welfare. Therefore no university on an inadequate budget should participate in any of the major intercollegiate sports, since all the major intercollegiate sports are costly and none is essential either to academic excellence or to the welfare of students.

($Ux = x$ is a university which operates on an inadequate budget, $Exy = x$ should engage in y, $Mx = x$ is expensive, $Ax = x$ is essential to academic excellence, $Wx = x$ is essential to student welfare, $Ix = x$ is a major intercollegiate sport)

314. Argument 109 presents reasoning to support the case of a coed who charged a fellow student with rape. Argument 314 is one of the arguments advanced on behalf of the boy.

The accused was an unarmed man. The accuser was an unbruised woman. If a man rapes a woman, then either he is armed or he overpowers her physically. If a man physically overpowers a woman she will have bruises. It follows that the accused did not rape his accuser.

($b =$ the accused, $Ax = x$ is armed, $Mx = x$ is a man, $c =$ the accuser, $Bx = x$ is bruised, $Wx = x$ is a woman, $Rxy = x$ rapes y, $Oxy = x$ overpowers y physically)

315. One statement entails a second if and only if it is logically impossible for the first to be true and the second false. For any two statements, if the second is logically true then it is logically impossible for the first to be true and the second false. This proves that a logically true statement is entailed by every statement.

(Universe of discourse: statements; $Exy = x$ entails y, $Ixy = $ it is logically impossible for x to be true and y false, $Lx = x$ is logically true) Argument 332 establishes the same point, but uses more complicated reasoning.

316.   One statement entails a second statement if and only if it
is logically impossible for the first to be true and the second false.
For any two statements, if the first is logically true and if it is
logically impossible for the first to be true and the second false,
then the second must be logically true also. So a logically true
statement does not entail any statements which are not logically
true.

(See 315.)

317. Some fundamentalists maintain that every descendent of Adam
possesses original sin. In order to escape attributing original sin to
Jesus they appeal to the doctrine of the virgin birth. However, as
317 shows, the virgin birth theory is not by itself sufficient to remove
Jesus from the scope of the fundamentalist claim about original
sin.[136]

Every descendent of Adam possesses original sin. Mary is a
descendent of Adam. Jesus is a descendent of Mary. "Descend-
ence" is a transitive relation.[137] Thus Jesus possessed original sin.

(Universe of discourse: persons; $Dxy = x$ is a descendent of y,
$a =$ Adam, $Ox = x$ possesses original sin, $m =$ Mary, $j =$ Jesus)

318. Philosophers of science are anxious to analyze the relationship
of *confirmation*—the relationship which exists between two statements when the first constitutes favorable evidence for the second.
It has been suggested that one statement confirms a second whenever the second entails the first. It has also been held that if one
statement confirms a second, then the first confirms any statement

---

[136] The Catholic doctrine of the immaculate conception of Mary is an
attempted resolution of this problem.
[137] See 372.

entailed by the second. Nelson Goodman shows[188] that these two claims taken together lead to absurdity.

> One statement confirms a second if and only if the second entails the first. If one statement confirms a second, then the first confirms any statement entailed by the second. For any two statements there exists at least one statement which entails both.[189] Therefore every statement confirms all statements.

(Universe of discourse: statements; $Cxy = x$ confirms y, $Exy = x$ entails y)

319. One of the arguments for the existence of God in Descartes' *Meditations*[140] may be set out in the following way.

> There is an idea of God. The idea of the more perfect cannot be the effect of the less perfect. Every idea has some cause. Anything which is not identical to God is less perfect than God. So God exists.

The second and third premises and the conclusion may be rephrased in this manner:

> If A is the idea of B and C causes A, then C is not less perfect than B. If A is the idea of B, then there is something which caused A. There exists something which is identical to God.

Notice how implausible the second premise is. ($Ixy = x$ is an idea of y, $g = $ God, $Lxy = x$ is less perfect than y, $Cxy = x$ causes y, $Axy = x$ is identical to y)

---

[188] See *Fact, Fiction, and Forecast*, pp. 67–68.
[139] E.g., the conjunction of the two statements.
[140] *Meditations on First Philosophy*, pp. 38–45.

320. Consider S1:

> (S1) There is a village which has a resident male barber who shaves all and only those male residents who do not shave themselves.

S1 is a logical contradiction; it is logically impossible that there be such a village.[141] On first consideration it is not obvious that this *is* a logical impossibility, so it is of interest to prove it. Argument 240 showed that any sentence which entails a contradiction is itself contradictory. Prove that S1 is contradictory by demonstrating that it entails S2, which is obviously contradictory:

> (S2) There is a barber who shaves himself although he does not shave himself.

($Vx = x$ is a village, $Rxy = x$ resides in y, $Mx = x$ is male, $Bx = x$ is a barber, $Sxy = x$ shaves y)

321. Gilbert Ryle rejects the view that the meaning of 'the first man to stand on the top of Mt. Everest' is Hillary.[142] (This view is an application of the "name" theory of meaning.)[143] He argues against this position as follows:

> No English phrase has a meaning which is a New Zealand citizen. Hillary is a citizen of New Zealand. Anything which is identical to a New Zealand citizen is also a New Zealand citizen. 'The first man to stand on the top of Mt. Everest' is an English phrase. This proves that the meaning of that phrase is not identical to Hillary.

[141] For a discussion of this and other paradoxes see W. V. Quine, "Paradox," *Scientific American*, CCVI (April, 1962), 84–96.
[142] "The Theory of Meaning," p. 245.
[143] See arguments 10, 11, 176, and 283.

($Ex = x$ is an English phrase, $Mxy = x$ is the meaning of y, $Nx = x$ is a New Zealand citizen, $h =$ Hillary, $Ixy = x$ is identical to y, $t =$ 'the first man to stand on the top of Mt. Everest')

322. In the dialogue *Theatetus*, Plato proves that the square root of a natural number is not a fraction.[144] Argument 322 paraphrases his reasoning.

> The square root of a perfect square is a natural number. No natural number is a fraction. The square root of a natural number other than a perfect square is not a fraction. Therefore the square root of a natural number is not a fraction.

($Rxy = x$ is the square root of y, $Px = x$ is a perfect square, $Nx = x$ is a natural number, $Fx = x$ is a fraction)

323. A particle of matter which is indivisible is not extended. Anything which lacks extension is nonmaterial. For any divisible particle of matter there is a second particle of matter which is smaller than the first. It follows that there are no smallest particles of matter.[145]

($Mx = x$ is material, $Dx = x$ is divisible, $Ex = x$ is extended, $Sxy = x$ is smaller than y)

324. For every integer there exists an integer which is the sum of the first integer and one. If one integer equals the sum of a second integer and one, then the two integers are different. "Identity" is a symmetrical relationship.[146] If one integer equals

---

[144] See Francis M. Cornford, *Plato's Theory of Knowledge*, pp. 22–23.
[145] Restated: it's not the case that there is something material such that nothing material is smaller than it.
[146] See 386.

the sum of a second integer and one, then the second is not larger than the first. This establishes that there does not exist an integer which is larger than all other (that is, nonidentical) integers.

(Universe of discourse: integers; $Sxy = x$ equals the sum of y and one, $Ixy = x$ is identical to y, $Lxy = x$ is larger than y)

325. Some logicians will say both of the following (although not in the same breath):

Any declarative-sentence meaning is a proposition.
Every proposition has a meaning.

Argument 325 shows that these two claims when combined with an obvious truth have a very peculiar consequence:

Any declarative-sentence meaning is a proposition. Every proposition has a meaning. Some declarative sentences have meanings. Hence there is something which is the meaning of the meaning of some declarative sentence.

($Dx = x$ is a declarative sentence, $Mxy = x$ is the meaning of y, $Px = x$ is a proposition)

326. In the *Meno*, Plato writes:

Socrates: I know, Meno, what you mean. . . . You argue that a man cannot enquire either about that which he knows, or about that which he does not know; for if he knows, he has no need to enquire; and if not, he cannot; for he does not know the very subject about which he is to enquire.[147]

---

[147] *The Dialogues of Plato*, I, 360.

This reasoning is paraphrased by 326.

> If one already knows a proposition, then one cannot come to know it. If, on the other hand, one does not already know a proposition, then one cannot recognize it as what one desired to know. And if one cannot recognize a proposition as that which he desired to know, then one cannot come to know it. It follows, then, that no one comes to know any proposition.

($Px = x$ is a person, $Kxy = x$ already knows y, $Ax = x$ is a proposition, $Cxy = x$ comes to know y, $Rxy = x$ recognizes y as that which x desired to know)

327. A deductive system is *complete* if and only if all the true formulas expressible in it are provable as theorems within the system. A deductive system is *consistent* if and only if there is a formula expressible in it which is not provable as a theorem within the system. Therefore every inconsistent deductive system is complete.

($Dx = x$ is a deductive system, $Ax = x$ is complete, $Tx = x$ is true, $Fx = x$ is a formula, $Exy = x$ is expressible in y, $Pxy = x$ is provable as a theorem in y, $Bx = x$ is consistent)

328. Any ampliative inference for which there is a cogent deductive justification is not an ampliative inference. Any nondeductive justification for an ampliative inference is viciously circular. Nothing which is viciously circular is cogent. Hence there is no cogent justification for any ampliative inference.[148]

---

[148] This is a paraphrase of Wesley Salmon's paraphrase of Hume's argument that induction cannot be justified. See Salmon's *The Foundations of Scientific Inference*, p. 11.

($Ax = x$ is an ampliative inference, $Cx = x$ is cogent, $Dx = x$ is deductive, $Jxy = x$ is a justification for y, $Vx = x$ is viciously circular)

329.   No school which has any black students should play Dixie, since a school should not play pep songs which any of its students find insulting, and Dixie is a pep song which every black person regards as an insult.[149]

($Ax = x$ is a school, $Bx = x$ is black, $Cxy = x$ is a student at y, $Pxy = x$ should play y, $d = Dixie$, $Ex = x$ is a pep song, $Ixy = x$ finds y insulting)

330. St. Thomas Aquinas' second cosmological argument for the existence of God may be interpreted as having the following structure:[150]

> Every entity in the sensible world has a cause. Any entity in the sensible world which is its own cause is prior to itself. No entity is prior to itself. If every entity in the sensible world has a cause, but does not cause itself, then[151] either there is an infinite series of causes or there is a first cause lying outside the sensible world. If there is an infinite series of causes, then there is no first cause. If there is no first cause, then there are no effects. But there are effects. (E) It follows that there is a first cause which lies outside the sensible world. (A)

---

[149] "The Valdosta, Ga., high-school band has devised a compromise to the conflict raging in many integrated schools in the South over the playing of 'Dixie.' The Valdosta band plays the battle hymn of the Confederacy in a medley that also includes 'We Shall Overcome.' " "Not Just Whistling Dixie," *Newsweek*, November 17, 1969, p. 31.

[150] See a selection from *Summa Theologica*, reprinted in Hick (ed.), *The Existence of God*, pp. 83–84. Compare with argument 143.

[151] From this point on 330 is truth-functional.

($Sx = x$ is in the sensible world, $Cxy = x$ causes y, $Pxy = x$ is prior to y, $I =$ There is an infinite series of causes, $A =$ There is a first cause lying outside the sensible world, $B =$ There is a first cause, E)

331. Given any two explanations for the same thing, if one is more probable than the other it is preferable to it. For any report of a miraculous occurrence, there is an explanation for the report which holds it to be false and which is more probable than any explanation of the report which does not take the report to be false. Hence for any miracle report there is an explanation of it which holds the report to be false and which is preferable to any explanation of the report which does not regard it as false.[152]

($Exy = x$ is an explanation for y, $Axy = x$ is more probable than y, $Bxy = x$ is preferable to y, $Mx = x$ is a miracle report, $Fxy = x$ holds y to be false)

332. If one statement entails a second, then any denial of the second entails any denial of the first. A contradiction entails all statements. Every logical truth is a denial of some contradiction. Every statement is a denial of some statement. Therefore a logically true statement is entailed by all statements.

(Universe of discourse: statements; Exy, $Dxy = x$ is a denial of y, $Cx = x$ is a contradiction, $Lx = x$ is a logical truth)

333. If a person knows a statement to be true must he also know to be true any statement which is entailed by the first one? The affirmative answer to this question leads to absurd consequences.

If a person knows a statement to be true, then he knows to be true any statement which is entailed by the first one. Every

---

[152] This is adapted freely from Hume, *An Inquiry Concerning Human Understanding*, section 10.

person who is not an infant knows at least one statement to be true. (As 332 proved) a logically true statement is entailed by every statement. It follows that every person past infancy knows every logically true statement to be true.

($Px = x$ is a person, $Kxy = x$ knows y to be true, $Sx = x$ is a statement, $Exy = x$ entails y, $Ix = x$ is an infant, $Lx = x$ is logically true)

334. No one is morally responsible for anything which is the inevitable consequence of something for which he is not morally responsible. Every adult engages in some actions which are the inevitable consequences of infantile situations. No adult is morally responsible for the situations in which he was placed as an infant. Consequently every adult commits some acts for which he is not morally responsible.[153]

($Rxy = x$ is morally responsible for y, $Cxy = x$ is the inevitable consequence of y, $Ax = x$ is an adult, $Exy = x$ engages in act y, $Sxy = x$ is a situation in which y was placed as an infant)

335. (DIFFICULT)

It is false that every valid deductive argument begs the question. Every valid deductive argument which has only one premise is such that it has a premise which by itself entails its conclusion. To every argument which has more than one premise there corresponds another argument which has only one premise,[154] and

---

[153] For a discussion of the topic treated by 334 see John Hospers' essay "What Means This Freedom?" in *Determinism and Freedom in the Age of Modern Science,* ed. by Sidney Hook.

[154] Namely, the argument which results from conjoining all of the premises of the original argument into one statement.

the first is deductively valid if and only if the second is. "Corresponding" is a symmetrical relationship.[155] So at least one of the following two claims is false: (1) every argument which has a premise which by itself entails its conclusion begs the question; (2) if one argument begs the question, then so does any corresponding argument.

(Universe of discourse: arguments; $Vx = x$ is deductively valid, $Bx = x$ begs the question, $Ox = x$ has only one premise, $Ex = x$ has a premise which by itself entails the conclusion of x, $Cxy = x$ corresponds to y)

336. (DIFFICULT) What is the nature of the inference from observational evidence to the scientific hypothesis which explains the evidence? It can be proved conclusively that the inference is not deductive.[156]

> For any observation statement and any hypothesis, there exists a second hypothesis which is logically compatible with the observation statement but not with the first hypothesis. "Logical compatibility" is a symmetrical relationship.[157] Any two statements are logically incompatible if and only if there exists a statement which is a denial of the second statement and is entailed by the first statement. "Entailment" is transitive.[158] All of this proves that no observation statement entails any hypothesis.

---

[155] See 386.
[156] This argument is found in Salmon, *The Foundations of Scientific Inference*, p. 19.
[157] See 386.
[158] See 372.

Notice that the second, third, and fourth premises are purely logical; their function is to facilitate the derivation of the conclusion from the first premise. (Universe of discourse: statements; $Ox = x$ is an observation statement, $Hx = x$ is an hypothesis, $Cxy = x$ is logically compatible with y, $Dxy = x$ is a denial of y, $Exy = x$ entails y)

337. (DIFFICULT) In Book Nine of his *Elements*,[159] Euclid proves that there are an infinite number of primes. His proof is summarized by 337. (Don't symbolize the parenthetical material.)

> If there exists a greatest prime, then there is a second number (namely, the sum of one and the product of all primes less than or equal to the greatest prime) which is greater than the greatest prime, and if this second number is not a prime, then (since every nonprime has a prime divisor) there exists a third number (a prime divisor of the second number) which is a prime and is greater than the greatest prime. (If this third number were identical to a prime smaller than or equal to the greatest prime, then it would be a divisor both of the second number and the number which is one less than the second number—which is impossible.) Therefore there is no greatest prime.

(Universe of discourse: numbers; $Gxy = x$ is greater than y, $Px = x$ is a prime)

338. (DIFFICULT)

> Every nonprime has a divisor which is not identical to one and such that no divisor of that nonprime other than one is less than that divisor. "Divisor of" is a transitive relation.[160] If

---

[159] *The Thirteen Books of Euclid's Elements,* trans. by Sir Thomas L. Heath, proposition 20.
[160] See 372.

one number is a divisor[161] of a second, then the first is smaller than the second. It follows that every nonprime has a prime divisor other than one.[162]

(Universe of discourse: numbers; $Px = x$ is a prime, $Dxy = x$ is a divisor of y, $Ix = x$ is identical to one, $Lxy = x$ is less than y)

339. (DIFFICULT) The philosopher P. F. Strawson[163] discusses a relationship holding between statements which he calls "presupposition." One statement *presupposes* a second when the first can have a truth value (that is, be either true or false) only if the second statement is true. For example, 'Scherer is a florist' *presupposes* 'Scherer exists.' A question arises: If one statement presupposes a second does it also entail the second? Strawson answers with an emphatic "no." A second philosopher, Leonard Linsky,[164] maintains that Strawson is wrong about this. I believe that 339 captures Linsky's reasoning.

If one statement presupposes another, then any statement claiming the first to have a truth value will entail any statement claiming that the second is true. For any statement there exists

---

[161] In this problem "divisor" must be understood to mean "number by which another *non-identical* number is divided"; otherwise the third premise is false.

[162] A less-compressed version of 338 runs as follows:

Consider any nonprime number, A. Since A is not a prime it has a divisor other than one. Let B be the smallest such divisor. B must be a prime number. Because if it is not, then it will have a divisor, C, which is less than B. Since C is a divisor of B and B a divisor of A, C will be a divisor of A. Therefore C is a divisor of A which is smaller than B, which is contrary to the hypothesis. Hence any nonprime, A, will have a prime divisor, B, which is not identical to one.

[163] See Strawson's *Introduction to Logical Theory*, p. 175.

[164] See Linsky's *Referring*, p. 94.

a second which claims the first to be true. For any statement there exists a second which claims the first to have a truth value. If one statement claims that a second is true and a third claims that the second has a truth value, then the first entails the third. "Entailment" is transitive. For any four statements, if the first claims the second to be true and the third claims the fourth to be true, then the first entails the third only if the second entails the fourth. Hence if one statement presupposes a second, then it also entails it.

(Universe of discourse: statements; $Pxy = x$ presupposes y, $Vxy = x$ claims y to have a truth value, $Txy = x$ claims y to be true, $Exy = x$ entails y)

340. (DIFFICULT) Some philosophers employ the concept of "volition" in order to handle certain difficult philosophical problems, notably the free-will problem. The volition theory, however, can easily lead to absurdities, as 340 shows.

Every free act is caused by a volition. Volitions are acts. No act caused by a nonfree volition is free. Therefore any volition which causes a free act is itself caused by a volition which in turn is caused by a volition.[165]

($Fx = x$ is free, $Ax = x$ is an act, $Cxy = x$ causes y, $Vx = x$ is a volition)

---

[165] The "chain" of volitions described in the conclusion may be lengthened indefinitely without destroying the validity of the argument.

7 | Valid and Invalid Relational Arguments

341.   Every event is caused by some event(s). Therefore there is an event which causes all events.

(Universe of discourse: events; $Cxy = x$ causes y)

342.   Every event is caused by some event(s). Hence every event causes some event(s).

(Universe of discourse: events; Cxy)

343. Evaluate 55 quantificationally. (a = Rachel, $Mxy = x$ is the mother of y, b = Richard, $Fxy = x$ is the father of y, c = Robert, $Gxy = x$ is the paternal grandmother of y)

344.   No one is a better quarterback than Joe Namath. So Namath is a better quarterback than anyone in the National Conference.

(Universe of discourse: persons; $Bxy = x$ is a better quarterback than y, j = Joe Namath, $Nx = x$ is in the National Conference)

345. In *The Republic,* Plato writes:

> There is something ridiculous in the expression
> "master of himself"; for the master is also the servant
> and the servant the master; and in all these modes of
> speaking the same person is denoted.[166]

Plato may be interpreted as advancing 345.

> If A is the master of B, then B is the servant of A. Therefore
> anyone who is master of himself is also servant of himself.

Is this argument valid? ($Mxy = x$ is master of y, $Sxy = x$ is servant of y)

346. Replace the conclusion of 344 with 'So Namath is at least as good a quarterback as anyone in the National Conference.' Evaluate the resulting inference. (See 344.)

347. The philosopher Peter Caws writes:

> . . . Taken as an element of a formal system, a sentence
> can be analytic only if the axioms from which it ulti-
> mately derives are analytic. Every proof in a formal
> system is analytic . . . but the theorem proved is not
> analytic unless the axioms are.[167]

Caws has committed a logical error. If the axioms of a consistent formal system are analytic, then the theorems must be analytic also; but it is false that if the *theorems* are analytic, the *axioms* must be analytic. The following miniature formal system is proof of this.

---

[166] *The Dialogues of Plato,* I, 694.
[167] *The Philosophy of Science,* p. 136.

AXIOMS: (A1) If it is snowing school will be cancelled.
                 (A2) If school will be cancelled it is snowing.
THEOREM: (T1) If it is snowing it is snowing.

Argument 347 drives the criticism home.

> T1 is derived from the axiom set composed of A1 and A2.
> T1 is analytic, but the axiom set is not. Therefore the claim that
> a theorem is analytic only if the axioms from which it derives are
> analytic is false.

($t = $ T1, $Dxy = x$ is a theorem derived from axiom set y, $a = $ the
axiom set composed of A1 and A2, $Ax = x$ is analytic)

348. One could arrive at the mistaken thesis mentioned in the preceding exercise by making the following inference. Is it valid?

> If one sentence is derived from a second, then if the second
> is analytic the first will also be analytic. Accordingly if one sen-
> tence is derived from a second, then the first will be analytic
> only if the second is also.

(Universe of discourse: sentences; $Dxy = x$ is derived from y,
$Ax = x$ is analytic)

349. Most deductive arguments which have only one premise are
either obviously valid or obviously invalid. Argument 349 is an
exception.

> Fred admires all persons who do not admire themselves. So
> Fred admires some self-admirer.

(Universe of discourse: persons; $f = $ Fred, $Axy = x$ admires y)

350.   If a person smokes he endangers his health—no matter what the substance smoked. It follows that people who smoke "pot" endanger their health.

($Px = x$ is a person, $Sxy = x$ smokes y, $Ex = x$ endangers his health, $Mx = x$ is "pot")

351. A headline in a newspaper ad says:

> Don't kid yourself!
> Your cigarette isn't lowest in "tar" unless it's lower than Carlton.

(We name the second sentence 'S.') S sounds impressive, but what does it actually mean? For example, does it logically imply that no cigarette has less "tar" than Carlton? Add this analytic auxiliary premise to 351 through 353:

> "Having less 'tar' than" is an asymmetric relation (that is, if one thing contains less "tar" than a second, then the second does not contain less "tar" than the first).

(Universe of discourse: cigarette brands; $a =$ your brand, $Lxy = x$ has less "tar" than y, $c =$ Carlton)

352. At the very least S must rule out Carlton's being highest in "tar." Does it? That is, does S entail 'There is a cigarette which has more "tar" than Carlton'? (See 351.)

353. Is it possible that S says no more than the following sentence (which is hardly favorable to Carlton)?

> If no cigarette has less "tar" than yours, then your cigarette is lower than Carlton.

Determine whether this sentence entails S. (See 351.)

354.   If a disjunction is not true, none of its disjuncts is true. Reason:
a disjunction is true only when at least one of its disjuncts is true.

($Ax = x$ is a disjunction, $Tx = x$ is true, $Bxy = x$ is a disjunct of y)

355. A relation is *intransitive* if and only if for any three (not
necessarily distinct) objects if the first bears the relation to the
second and the second bears the relation to the third, then the first
fails to bear the relation to the third.[168] "Being two inches taller than"
is an intransitive relation. The logician E. J. Lemmon says that
"being parent of" is an intransitive relation.[169] Argument 355 purports to show that he is mistaken.[170]

Jocasta was a parent of Oedipus. Jocasta and Oedipus were
parents of Polynices. So it is false that "being parent of" is an
intransitive relation.[171]

(Universe of discourse: persons; $j = $ Jocasta, $Pxy = x$ is a parent
of y, $o = $ Oedipus, $p = $ Polynices)

356. During the Last Supper (according to the account in Matthew[172]), Jesus said to his disciples, "Truly, I say to you, as you did

---

[168] Compare intransitivity with transitivity. See 372.
[169] *Beginning Logic*, p. 183.
[170] The expression 'parent of' is ambiguous; it can denote either a biological relation or a legal relation. Is either relation intransitive? Is the
biological relation "father of" intransitive? How about the legal relation?
[171] In other words, it is false that if one person is a parent of a second
and the second is a parent of a third, then the first is not a parent of the
third.
[172] See Matthew 25: 31–46.

it to one of the least of these my brethren, you did it to me." Somewhat later in his speech he also said, "Truly, I say to you, as you did it not to one of the least of these, you did it not to me." Was the second statement merely a repetition, perhaps for emphasis, of the first statement, or did it introduce a new thought? Rephrased, is 356 valid or invalid?

> Anyone who helps an unfortunate person helps Jesus. Thus anyone who helps no unfortunate persons does not help Jesus.

(Universe of discourse: persons; $Hxy = x$ helps y, $Ux = x$ is unfortunate, $j = $ Jesus)

357.   The earth does not rotate from west to east. (R) Proof: If it does rotate from west to east, then anything which is dropped from a tower should land to the west of the tower. However nothing dropped from a tower behaves in this way.

(R, $Dxy = x$ is dropped from y, $Tx = x$ is a tower, $Wxy = x$ lands to the west of y)

358.   If the first premise of 357 is true, then any fly who left the dashboard of a speeding car would be smashed against the back window of the car. There are flies which have left the dashboard of a speeding car and have not been smashed against the rear window. Therefore the first premise of 357 is not correct. (P)

(P, $Fx = x$ is a fly, $Lxy = x$ leaves the dashboard of y, $Cx = x$ is a speeding car, $Sxy = x$ is smashed against the back window of y)

359. Supplement the premise set of 357 with 'Something has been dropped from some tower,' and reevaluate the argument. (See 357.)

360. A radio commercial claims "The more carefully a beer is brewed the better it tastes; and Schlitz is the most carefully brewed beer in the world." This is an argument with a suppressed (unstated) conclusion. What is the conclusion which the brewer wants you to draw? Does that conclusion follow from the two premises given? (Universe of discourse: beers; $Cxy = x$ is brewed more carefully than y, $Txy = x$ tastes better than y, $s =$ Schlitz, $Ixy = x$ is identical to y)

361. In *Language, Truth and Logic*,[173] A. J. Ayer says 'The difference in type between philosophical and scientific propositions is such that they cannot conceivably contradict one another.' The falsity of this is a consequence of another of Ayer's views (namely, that philosophical propositions are analytic) taken together with some obvious truths.

> All philosophical propositions are analytic. At least one philosophical proposition is false. A false analytic proposition contradicts every proposition. This establishes the falsity of the claim that no philosophical proposition contradicts any scientific proposition.

(Universe of discourse: propositions; $Px = x$ is philosophical, $Ax = x$ is analytic, $Fx = x$ is false, $Cxy = x$ contradicts y, $Sx = x$ is scientific)

362.
> In any valid syllogism no term is distributed in the conclusion unless it is also distributed in a premise. Any syllogism in mood EOI has at least one term which is distributed in a premise but is not distributed in the conclusion. Hence any syllogism whose mood is EOI is invalid.

(Vx, $Sx = x$ is a syllogism, $Txy = x$ is a term in y, $Cxy = x$ is distributed in the conclusion of y, $Pxy = x$ is distributed in a premise of y, $Ex = x$ is in mood EOI)

---

[173] P. 57.

363. Add 'There is at least one scientific proposition' to the premise set of 361 and reevaluate it. (See 361.)

364. How is the mathematical truth 'There is no largest number' to be symbolized? S1 and S2 are two possible first steps in producing a formula:

(S1) For any x there exists a y such that y is greater than x.
(S2) It is not the case that there exists an x such that for any y, x is greater than y.

Are S1 and S2 logically equivalent? They are if and only if 364 and 365 are both valid. (In both arguments include this analytic auxiliary premise: ' "Greater than" is an asymmetric relation.' See 351.)

S1. Therefore S2.

(Universe of discourse: numbers; $Gxy = x$ is greater than y)

365.   **S2. Therefore S1.**

(See 364.)

366. Since S1 and S2 (see 364) are not logically equivalent, at least one of them must be an incorrect rendering of 'There is no largest number.' We could prove that S2 is a mistaken translation by showing that it follows from a statement which would be true even if there were a largest number. If S2 would be true even if 'There is no largest number' were false, then the two sentences do not say the same thing. If 366 is valid, S2 is a mistaken translation of 'There is no largest number.'

> No number is greater than itself. Thus S2.

(See 364.)

367. Does the criticism leveled above against S2 apply also to S1? That is, is 367 valid?

> No number is greater than itself. Hence S1.

(See 364.)

368. Berkeley advances an argument for the existence of God which is based on his philosophical position.[174]

> Every sense idea has some cause. Nothing exists except what is either spirit or idea. Ideas do not cause anything. Therefore there is a spirit (God) who causes all sense ideas.

($Ax = x$ is a sense idea, $Cxy = x$ causes y, $Sx = x$ is a spirit, $Ix = x$ is an idea)

369. An advertising jingle goes: "Everybody doesn't like something, but nobody doesn't like Sara Lee." Suppose we change the 'something' to 'someone' and make the assumption that Sara Lee is a person (rather than a line of bakery goods). Would the jingle so revised contradict the thesis that if one person likes a second, the second will reciprocate? That is, is argument 369 valid?

> Everybody doesn't like someone, but nobody doesn't like

---

[174] *The Principles of Human Knowledge*, pp. 35–38.

> Sara Lee. So it is false that "liking" is a symmetrical relation-ship.[175]

(Universe of discourse: persons; $Lxy = x$ likes y, $s =$ Sara Lee)

370. Replace the conclusion of 368 with 'Therefore every sense idea is caused by some spirit,' and test the resulting argument. (See 368.)

371. A philosopher friend of mine hoped to prove that at least one desire of each person ought to be satisfied. His argument consisted in disproving the thesis that no desires of anyone should be satisfied. Did he make his case? That is, is 371 valid?

> It is false that no desires of any person ought to be satisfied. So at least one desire of each person ought to be satisfied.

($Dxy = x$ is a desire of y, $Px = x$ is a person, $Sx = x$ ought to be satisfied)

372. A relation is "transitive" if and only if for any three (not necessarily distinct) objects if the first bears the relation to the second and the second to the third, then the first bears the relation to the third. "Being taller than" is a transitive relation. "Being brother of," on the other hand, is not. Each of the next two arguments attempts to establish that the brother relation isn't transitive.

> Someone is the brother of someone. But no one is his own brother. This shows that "being brother of" is not a transitive relation.[176]

---

[175] See 386.

[176] In other words, this shows the falsity of the claim that if one person

(Universe of discourse: persons; $Bxy = x$ is brother of y)

373.   There are two persons such that each is brother of the other. But since no one is his own brother, "being brother of" cannot be a transitive relation.

(See 372.)

374. If the philosopher mentioned in 371 disproved the thesis that there is someone none of whose desires ought to be satisfied, would he have made out his case? That is, is 374 valid?

It is false that there is someone none of whose desires ought to be satisfied. So at least one desire of each person ought to be satisfied.

(See 371.)

375. Proposition XIII of Part I of Spinoza's *Ethics* is 'Substance absolutely infinite is indivisible.' Spinoza's proof for this proposition may be paraphrased as follows:[177]

If infinite substance is divisible, then if all of its parts are also infinite, there are (at least) two substances which have the same nature. But no two substances have the same nature. (S) If infinite substance is divisible, then if none of its parts is infinite, then all of them can cease to exist. If infinite substance is divisible and all of its parts can cease to exist, then infinite substance itself can cease to exist. However, infinite substance cannot cease to exist. Therefore infinite substance is not divisible.

---

is brother of a second and the second is brother of a third, then the first is brother of the third.

[177] See *The Chief Works of Benedict de Spinoza*, trans. by R. H. M. Elwes, II, 54.

(i = infinite substance, $Dx = x$ is divisible, $Pxy = x$ is a part of y, $Ix = x$ is infinite, S = There are two substances which have the same nature, $Cx = x$ can cease to exist)

376. Consider this definition of 'humility':

> A person is humble if and only if he does not admire himself.

Is it a logical consequence of this definition that no humble person admires all humble persons? (Universe of discourse: persons; $Hx = x$ is humble, $Axy = x$ admires y)

377. Add 'If infinite substance is divisible, then it is false that some of its parts are infinite and some are not infinite' to the premise set of 375 and evaluate the resulting argument. (See 375.)

378. Does Lincoln's famous aphorism

> It is true that you may fool all the people some of the time; you can even fool some of the people all the time; but you can't fool all of the people all the time[178]

entail 'There is a person such that some of the time he can be fooled and some of the time he can't be fooled'? ($Fxy = x$ can be fooled at y, $Px = x$ is a person, $Tx = x$ is a moment of time)

379. The first clause in Lincoln's aphorism (see 378) is ambiguous. It could mean either S1 or S2:

> (S1) There are times when you may fool all the people.
> (S2) You may fool any person some of the time.

---

[178] John Bartlett, *Familiar Quotations*, p. 542.

Is there a significant difference between these two interpretations or do they make the same claim? For instance, does S2 entail S1? (See 378.)

380. A relation is "reflexive" if and only if every object which enters into the relation bears the relation to itself. "Entailment" is such a relation. Two formal descriptions of reflexivity have been suggested:

> (D1) For any two objects, if the first bears R to the second, then the first bears R to itself and the second bears R to itself.
>
> (D2) For any two objects, if either the first bears R to the second or the second bears R to the first, then the first bears R to itself.

Do these two statements say the same thing or is one of them weaker than the other? Find out by testing 380 and 381.

D1. Therefore D2.

(Rxy)

381.   **D2. Therefore D1.**

(Rxy)

382. How are scientific terms ending in 'able,' 'uble,' 'ible,' etc.—so-called "disposition terms"—to be defined? Consider 'soluble' as an example. One suggested definition is:

> (D1) A thing is soluble if and only if it dissolves whenever it is put into water.

This definition has been criticized on the grounds that it has the following absurd consequence:

Everything which is never placed in water is soluble.

Does D1 entail this statement? ($Sx = x$ is soluble, $Dxy = x$ dissolves at time y, $Wxy = x$ is placed in water at time y)

383. The philosopher Rudolf Carnap has suggested an alternative definition of 'soluble':[179]

(D2) If a thing is put into water at any time, then it is soluble if and only if it dissolves at that time.

Does D2 entail the absurdity that everything which is never placed in water is soluble? (Wxy, Sx, Dxy)

384. Definitions like D2 (see 383) have a characteristic which is unusual for definitions, namely, they have empirical content.[180] The proof of this is that two such sentences taken together can entail an empirical sentence. (If a consistent set of sentences entails an empirical sentence, then the set is also empirical. See 391.) Argument 384 provides an example of this.

If a thing is close to a small iron object, then it is magnetic if and only if the iron object moves toward it. If a thing moves

---

[179] See "Testability and Meaning," in *Readings in the Philosophy of Science*, ed. by Herbert Feigl and May Brodbeck, p. 53. D2 is called a "partial definition" since it gives a meaning to 'soluble' only in reference to objects placed in water.

[180] This has been noted by the philosopher Carl Hempel in *Fundamentals of Concept Formation in Empirical Science*, International Encyclopedia of Unified Science, Vol. II, No. 7, pp. 27–28.

through a closed wire loop, then it is magnetic if and only if it generates an electric current in the loop. From these it follows that anything which is near a small iron object and is moving through a closed wire loop will generate an electric current in the loop if and only if the small iron object moves toward it.

($Nxy = x$ is near small iron object y, $Mx = x$ is magnetic, $Txy = x$ moves toward y, $Lxy = x$ moves through closed wire loop y, $Gxy = x$ generates an electric current in y)

385. Mike's favorite toy is a bank which has a green hand that grabs coins placed in a slot. When the bank stopped operating, Mike (age: 3) demanded an explanation, which went like this: "The penny box won't work now because it needs new batteries, and we won't have those batteries until we go to the Super–X." The explanation could be formalized as follows:

The penny box will not work until we go to the Super–X, because (1) it won't work until we put new batteries into it, (2) we can't put new batteries into it before we go to the Super–X, and (3) if one moment of time is earlier than a second, then for any third moment either the first is earlier than it or it is earlier than the second.

($Px = x$ is a time when the penny box is working, $Exy =$ time x is earlier than time y, $Sx = x$ is the time when we go to the Super–X, $Bx = x$ is the time when we put new batteries into the penny box)

386. A relation is "symmetrical" if and only if for any two objects, if the first bears the relation to the second, then the second bears it to the first. "Being a teammate of" is such a relation. Argument 386 tries to prove that any relation which is both symmetrical and transitive (see 372) is also reflexive (see 380).

Relation R is symmetrical. It is also transitive. So it is reflexive.

(Rxy)

387. Add 'There is a time when we put new batteries into the penny box' to the premise set of 385 and reevaluate it. (See 385.)

388. Why is 385 invalid? Because it is possible for all three premises to be true while the conclusion is false. Suppose that we never put new batteries into the penny box. This automatically makes the first two premises true. Prove that this is so; that is, prove that the following is valid:

> We never put new batteries into the penny box. Therefore the penny box won't work until we put new batteries into it, and we can't put new batteries into it before we go to the Super–X.

(See 385.) The third premise is analytically true by virtue of the meaning of 'earlier.' Suppose that the penny box starts to work again before we go to the Super–X (the old batteries are somehow revitalized). Under this supposition (which is compatible with the truth of the premises) the conclusion of 385 is false. Hence the argument is invalid.

389. A familiar commercial proclaims:

> When you're out of Schlitz, you're out of beer!

What is the logical content of this statement? The advertisers would like us to believe that the statement entails 'All (*real*) beer is Schlitz.' Does it? ($Tx = x$ is a time, $Px = x$ is a person, $Hxyz = x$ has y at z, $Sx = x$ is Schlitz, $Bx = x$ is beer)

390. Is the statement in the Schlitz ad (see previous exercise) entailed by 'All beer is Schlitz'? (See 389.)

391. A consistent set of sentences is either empirical or logically true. If it is logically true, then it does not entail any empirical sentences. Hence if a consistent set of sentences entails an empirical sentence, then the set is also empirical.

($Cx = x$ is a consistent set of sentences, $Ex = x$ is empirical, $Sx = x$ is a sentence, $Lx = x$ is logically true, $Axy = x$ entails y)

392. Several graduate students in the philosophy department at the University of Miami and I met with executives of Dow Latin America (whose headquarters are in Greater Miami) to discuss the morality of producing napalm.[181] The Dow officials denied that they manufactured napalm in order to make money, and claimed that the company was morally obligated to supply the government with napalm. In support of this claim they advanced the following argument:

If a firm is asked by its government to supply that government with war materials which are needed by its soldiers, then the company is morally obligated to sell those materials to the government unless the government is nondemocratic. Dow is a company under the U. S. Government, which is a democracy. The U. S. Government has asked Dow to supply it with napalm. Napalm is a war material which is needed by U. S. soldiers. So Dow is morally obligated to sell napalm to the U. S. Government.

($Cx = x$ is a company, $Gxy = x$ is under government y, $Axyz = x$ asks y to supply x with z, $Wx = x$ is a war material, $Nxy =$ the

---

181 Rocky Walters (see 1 and 191) arranged the meeting.

soldiers of x need y, $Oxyz = x$ is obligated to sell y to z, $Dx = x$ is democratic, $d = Dow$, $u =$ the U. S. Government, $n =$ napalm)

393. The weakest link in 392 is the first premise. When the philosophy students pointed this out, the Dow executives were unable to provide any support for the premise. That premise could be attacked in this way:

> No company is morally obligated to sell to its government any war materials which are outlawed by the Geneva Convention.[182] Consequently, it is false that if a firm is asked by its government to supply that government with war materials which are needed by its soldiers, then the company is morally obligated to sell those materials to the government unless the government is nondemocratic.

(Cx, $Oxyz$, Gxy, Wx, $Bx = x$ is outlawed by the Geneva Convention, $Axyz$, Nxy, Dx)

394. A second attack on the first premise of 392:

> It is not true that if the soldiers of a democratic government needed war materials which are outlawed by the Geneva Convention, then any company under that government which was asked by the government to supply these materials would be morally obligated to sell them to the government. So it is false that if a firm is asked by its government to supply that government with war materials which are needed by its soldiers, then the company is morally obligated to sell those materials to the government unless the government is nondemocratic.

(See 393.)

---

[182] This argument does not imply that napalm is outlawed by the Geneva Convention.

395. (DIFFICULT) Leibniz defines "the good man" as "one who loves all men as much as reason allows." [183] Does it follow from this definition (without the qualification about reason) that there is a person who loves all good persons? That is, is 395 valid?

A person is good if and only if he loves everybody. Hence there is a person who loves all good persons.

(Universe of discourse: persons; $Gx = x$ is good, $Lxy = x$ loves y)

---

[183] *Leibniz Selections*, p. 559.

8
Arguments in Their Natural Habitat[184]

396. "One may well ask, 'How can you advocate breaking some laws and obeying others?' The answer is found in the fact that there are two types of laws: There are *just* laws and there are *unjust* laws. I would be the first to advocate obeying just laws. One has not only a legal but a moral responsibility to obey just laws. Conversely, one has a moral responsibility to disobey unjust laws. I would agree with Saint Augustine that 'An unjust law is no law at all.'

"Now what is the difference between the two? How does one determine when a law is just or unjust? A just law is a man-made code that squares with the moral law or the law of God. An unjust law is a code that is out of harmony with the moral law. To put it in the terms of Saint Thomas Aquinas, an unjust law is a human law that is not rooted in eternal and natural law. Any law that uplifts human personality is just. Any law that degrades human personality is unjust.

"All segregation statutes are unjust because segregation distorts the soul and damages the personality. . . ."

---

[184] All of the copyrighted passages in this section are reprinted by permission.

Martin Luther King, Jr., "Letter from Birmingham City Jail," *The New Leader,* June 24, 1963, p. 6.

397. "Not all soil animals are beneficial. Some beetle and fly larvae are serious crop pests." [185]

> From "Soil Pollutants and Soil Animals" by Clive A. Edwards. Copyright © 1969 by Scientific American, Inc. All rights reserved. April, 1969, p. 88.

398. "The most valuable of all the soil invertebrates to man is probably the earthworm; these animals break down much of the plant debris reaching the soil and also turn over the soil and aerate it. Accordingly pesticide residues in soils that appreciably reduce the numbers of earthworms are a particularly serious matter."

> *Ibid.,* p. 92.

399. "*Union Man:* We saw you on television [during the 1968 Democratic convention], Senator, and it seemed like you were for those hippies. You're not getting our vote this time.

"*Ribicoff:* Look, suppose your kid was beaten up by the cops, how would you feel?

"*Union Man:* Those hippies the cops beat up were wearing beards and anybody who wears a beard, he deserves to get beat up."

> Quoted by Stewart Alsop in "Nixon and the New Bourgeoisie," *Newsweek,* January 27, 1969, p. 96.

400. "*Union Man:* . . . Anybody who wears a beard, he deserves to get beat up.

---

[185] Many arguments in this section are enthymemes (arguments which have unstated premises); 397 is such an argument. An enthymeme's missing premises must be supplied before it can be assessed.

"Ribicoff: Christ wore a beard. Abraham Lincoln wore a beard."

Ibid.

401. "Common sense says everything that happens is caused. It follows that everything I do must be caused, for among the things that happen in the universe are the actions that I perform."

> James W. Cornman and Keith Lehrer, *Philosophical Problems and Arguments: An Introduction,* p. 123. Copyright ©, The Macmillan Company, 1968.

402. "Word spread around Tony's Fish Market that Adam Clayton Powell or his double was having dinner. Tony Sweet asked if the man made a reservation and if he showed up on time. The hostess said yes. 'Then it's not Powell,' said Tony."

> Herb Kelly, *The Miami News,* July 24, 1968, p. 5–B.

403. "The determinist view seems to be the most adequate. He says that if all actions are caused then no actions are free and no actions are free, therefore everything is caused."

> From a mid-term examination in Introduction to Philosophy, University of Miami, March 25, 1969.

404. "[Ramsey reasoned:] . . . Since all propositions are statements of atomic fact, or reducible to such, and since general propositions are not reducible to such, therefore they are not genuine propositions at all."

> J. O. Urmson, *Philosophical Analysis: Its Development Between the Two World Wars* (Oxford: The Clarendon Press, 1956), p. 67. Reprinted by permission of Oxford University Press.

405. "QUESTION OF THE WEEK: DO YOU THINK THAT MARIJUANA SHOULD BE LEGALIZED?

"Richard Soll—'Yes, I think that marijuana should be legalized because there has never been any evidence to prove it harmful, therefore, people should not be arrested for the use of it.' "

"Student Controversy—Legalizing Marijuana," *The Miami Hurricane*, October 8, 1968, p. 8.

406. "Hereby it is manifest, that during the time men live without a common power to keep them all in awe, they are in that condition which is called war; and such a war, as is of every man, against every man. . . .

"To this war of every man against every man, this also is consequent; that nothing can be unjust. The notions of right and wrong, justice and injustice have there no place. Where there is no common power, there is no law: where no law, no injustice."

Thomas Hobbes, *Leviathan* (Chicago: Henry Regnery Co., 1956), pp. 118–20.

407. "For animal meat to be kosher the animal has to have split hooves and chew its cud. The pig does not chew its cud so it is not kosher, or 'terefah.' "

Bob Wilcox, "Keeping Kosher: A Serious Matter," *The Miami News,* January 15, 1970, p. 7–C.

408. "I *do* know that this pencil exists; but I could not know this, if Hume's principles were true; *therefore*, Hume's principles, one or both of them, are false."

George Edward Moore, *Some Main Problems of Philosophy* (London: George Allen & Unwin, Ltd., 1953), pp. 119–20. Reprinted by permission of the publisher.

409.

October 8, 1968, King Features Syndicate, Inc.

410.

April 21, 1969, King Features Syndicate, Inc.

411.

January 7, 1969, King Features Syndicate, Inc.

412.

October 23, 1968, © 1968, Publishers-Hall Syndicate and Daily Mirror, London TM®.

413.

December 17, 1969, Washington Star Syndicate, Inc.

414.

December 23, 1968, Washington Star Syndicate, Inc.

415.

December 31, 1968, Washington Star Syndicate, Inc.

416.

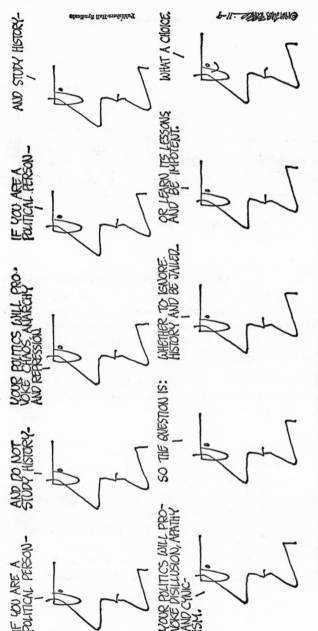

417.

February 25, 1969. By permission of Johnny Hart and Field Enterprises, Inc.

418. "In general, if you think I am mistaken in my belief, you will deny that I know, no matter how sincere you judge me to be and no matter how strong you consider my conviction. For X to be judged mistaken is sufficient basis for rejecting the claim that he knows. It follows that if X is admitted to know, he must be judged not to be mistaken. . . ."

> Israel Scheffler, *Conditions of Knowledge: An Introduction to Epistemology and Education* (Glenview, Ill.: Scott, Foresman & Company, 1965), p. 23.

419. "Everybody wins except Joe Robbie.

"Upon his signing cornerback Jimmy Warren and linebacker Wahoo McDaniel to contracts yesterday . . . , Miami Dolphin president Robbie was told laughingly he was getting a reputation as a 'soft touch' among the players.

"Robbie has stepped in to satisfy recalcitrants often this year when negotiations seemed stuck.

"'I'm a tightwad if I don't sign a guy and I'm an easy mark if I do,' he grinningly replied in an 'I-can't-win' tone."

"I Just Can't Win, Dolphin Boss Says," *The Miami News*, September 14, 1968, p. 1-B.

420. "The phrase 'what such and such an expression means' does not describe a thing or happening at all, and *a fortiori* not an occult thing or happening [that is, a thought]."

> Gilbert Ryle, *The Concept of Mind* (New York: Barnes & Noble, Inc., 1949), p. 295. Reprinted by permission of the author, Hutchinson & Co., Ltd., and Barnes & Noble, Inc.

421. "The seemingly simple problem of pulling telephone wires through conduit has important economic implications. In large buildings, for example, we would like to add more wires in existing conduits as the need for communications services grows. But friction between the wires eventually prevents more from being drawn through. Then, a new conduit must be installed, even though the previous one is not really full. What is needed is slippery wire.

"Recently, Bell Laboratories and Western Electric greatly increased the useful capacity of conduits by developing a new low-friction polyvinyl insulation for the Bell System's general-purpose wire. Since the new wire slides more easily, it needs less tensile strength, and so it can be smaller."

> Bell Systems advertisement, *Scientific American*, CCXX (April, 1969), 13.

422. (Continuation of preceding passage)
"We did several things to make the new wire more slippery.
". . . We made the jacket rougher—not smoother. . . . Smooth surfaces lead to more intimate contact and, therefore, more friction."

> *Ibid.*

423. "A paradox arises when two equally evident assumptions lead to apparently inconsistent results. A paradox is, therefore, rationally intolerable. No rational man can accept inconsistent results; consequently, no rational man can tolerate a paradox."

> James W. Cornman and Keith Lehrer, *Philosophical Problems and Arguments: An Introduction*, p. 120. Copyright ©, The Macmillan Company, 1968.

424. "If Utilitarianism be true it would be one's duty to try to increase the numbers of a community, even though one reduced the average total happiness of the members, so long as the total happiness in the community would be in the least increased. It seems perfectly plain to me that this kind of action, so far from being a duty, would quite certainly be wrong."

> C. D. Broad, *Five Types of Ethical Theory* (London: Routledge & Kegan Paul, 1930), p. 250. Reprinted by permission of Routledge & Kegan Paul, Ltd., and Humanities Press, Inc. (New York).

425. "Now if Christ is preached as raised from the dead, how can some of you say that there is no resurrection of the dead? But if there is no resurrection of the dead, then Christ has not been raised. . . .

"But in fact Christ has been raised from the dead, the first fruits of those who have fallen asleep."

> I Corinthians 15:12, 13, and 20. From the Revised Standard Version of the Bible, copyrighted 1946 and 1952, and used by permission.

426. "No sort of referential theory will be adequate as a general account of meaning unless it is true that all meaningful linguistic expressions do refer to something. And if we take a careful look at the matter, it will be seen that this is not the case."

William Alston, *Philosophy of Language* (Englewood Cliffs, N. J.: Prentice-Hall, Inc., 1964), p. 14.

427. "To resolve the conflict, it has been tempting to adopt a policy of peaceful co-existence, and divide our experience into two parts, granting science control over one part, and permitting religion its authority in the other.

"Let science investigate the physical world while religion explains spiritual matters, this argument goes. When science gets to the end of its rope, let faith take over to account for the unexplainable.

"This is a fatal step. Two separate worlds for science and religion might work if no scientist were ever a Christian, and no Christian were ever a scientist. But science and religion do not operate in separate realms."

> Wernher Von Braun, "Science Is Helping to Put Face on God" (North American Newspaper Alliance), *The Miami News*, August 6, 1966, p. 4–A.

428. "Scientists now believe that in nature, matter cannot be destroyed without being converted into energy. Not even the tiniest particle can disappear without a trace. Nature does not know extinction—only transformation. Would God have less regard for His masterpiece of creation, the human soul?"

> *Ibid.*

429. "The moral 'ought' implies 'can.' If we say that A morally ought to have done X, we imply that in our opinion, he could have done X. But we assign moral blame to a man only for failing to do what we think he morally ought to have done. Hence if we morally blame A for not having done X, we imply that he could have done X even though in fact he did not."

C. A. Campbell, "Is 'Free Will' a Pseudo-Problem?" *Mind,* LX (1951), 451.

430. "*Socrates.* And now, Laches, do you try and tell me in like manner, What is that common quality which is called courage . . . ?

"*Laches.* I should say that courage is a sort of endurance of the soul, if I am to speak of the universal nature which pervades [all cases of courage].

"*Soc.* But that is what we must do if we are to answer the question. And yet I cannot say that every kind of endurance is, in my opinion, to be deemed courage. Hear my reason: I am sure, Laches, that you would consider courage to be a very noble quality.

"*La.* Most noble, certainly.

"*Soc.* And you would say that a wise endurance is also good and noble?

"*La.* Very noble.

"*Soc.* But what would you say of a foolish endurance? Is not that, on the other hand, to be regarded as evil and hurtful?

"*La.* True.

"*Soc.* And is anything noble which is evil and hurtful?

"*La.* I ought not to say that, Socrates.

"*Soc.* Then you would not admit that sort of endurance to be courage—for it is not noble, but courage is noble?

"*La.* You are right."

Plato, "Laches," in *The Dialogues of Plato,* trans. by B. Jowett, 2 vols. (New York: Random House, 1892), I, 67–68.

431. "Tiny Tim: . . . I can never get married! Because I can never be faithful because if I'm looking, I'm dreaming; and if I'm dreaming, I'm wishing; and I could never stay married like that."

Dick Hobson, "Clark Kent, After All, Can Turn into Superman," *TV Guide,* October 12, 1968, pp. 45–46. Reprinted from TV

432. "The central point of the theory of descriptions was that a phrase may contribute to the meaning of a sentence without having any meaning at all in isolation. Of this, in the case of descriptions, there is precise proof: If 'the author of *Waverley*' meant anything other than 'Scott', 'Scott is the author of *Waverley*' would be false, which it is not. If 'the author of *Waverley*' meant 'Scott', 'Scott is the author of *Waverley*' would be a tautology, which it is not. Therefore, 'the author of *Waverley*' means neither 'Scott' nor anything else—i.e., 'the author of *Waverley*' means nothing, Q.E.D."

Bertrand Russell, *My Philosophical Development* (New York: Simon and Schuster, Inc., 1959), p. 85. Reprinted by permission of George Allen & Unwin, Ltd., and Simon & Schuster, Inc.

433. "He [Danelia] claims that he got the idea for 'Meet Me in Moscow' from a screenwriter who 'once told me that during a rainstorm he saw a girl running barefoot and a boy on a bicycle trying to shield her with an umbrella.' Any director who sets out to make a feature film because of a barefoot girl and a boy on a bike is either a simpleton or a poet, and Danelia is no simpleton."

Newsweek, February 14, 1966, p. 94.

434. "We reject the subjectivist view that to call an action right, or a thing good, is to say that it is generally approved of, because it is not self-contradictory to assert that some actions which are generally approved of are not right, or that some things which are generally approved of are not good."

From *Language, Truth and Logic* by Alfred Jules Ayer, Dover Publications, Inc., New York, 1952, p. 104. Reprinted through permission of the publisher and Victor Gollancz Ltd.

435. "DEAR ABBY:

"May I share my happiness with the world? I threw away my girdle about two months ago, and now I am free, free, free! I can't understand how I ever put up with that uncomfortable harness for so many years.

"Now I just slip into a pair of pantyhose and I'm ready to go! What a time saver! It used to take me 20 minutes to struggle into my girdle.

                                                         FREE AGAIN

"DEAR FREE:

"Congratulations. I'd have to see you before sharing your enthusiasm. Any woman who needs 20 minutes to 'struggle' into a girdle, needs one."

Abigail Van Buren, "Dear Abby" (Chicago Tribune–New York News Syndicate, Inc.), *The Miami News*, August 14, 1969, p. 22–D.

436. "DEAR ABBY:

"I am planning my Sweet 16 party and have run into a problem. My best girl friend is going with a boy who, quite frankly, I can't stand. I want her, but not him. Should I invite them both, or just my girl friend?

                                                    PLANNING MY PARTY

"DEAR PLANNING:

"You'll not have a 'successful' party unless all the guests have a good time. If you don't invite your best friend's boyfriend, she won't have any fun.

"Invite him. At age 16, it's time you learned to 'stand' people you 'can't stand' occasionally to please good friends."

Abigail Van Buren, "Dear Abby" (Chicago Tribune–New York News Syndicate, Inc.), *The Miami News,* April 21, 1969, p. 8–B.

437. "DEAR FEELING:

"Ten years later is pretty darned late to remember that a rug is an heirloom. If the woman valued your friendship she wouldn't have suggested such a thing [selling the rug]."

Ann Landers, "Dear Ann" (Publishers-Hall Syndicate), *Atlanta Journal,* June 20, 1969, p. 6–B.

438. (Continuation of preceding passage)
"If you don't sell the rug back to her for what you paid, her nose will be out of joint. If you do, yours will be. Take your choice."

Ibid.

439. "First, we must know that all substances in general—that is to say, all those things which cannot exist without being created by God—are by nature incorruptible and can never cease to be, unless God himself, by denying them his usual support, reduces them to nothingness. And secondly, we must notice that body, taken in general, is a substance, and that it therefore will never perish. But the human body, however much it may differ from other bodies, is only a composite, produced by a certain configuration of members and by other similar accidents, whereas the human soul is not thus dependent upon any accidents, but is a pure substance. For even if all its accidents change—as, for example, if it conceives of certain things, wills others, and receives sense impressions of still others—nevertheless it still remains the same soul. But the human body becomes a different entity from the mere fact that the shape of some of its parts has been changed. From this it follows that the human body may very easily perish, but that the mind or soul of man, between which I find no distinction, is immortal by its very nature."

Réné Descartes, *Meditations on First Philosophy* (Indianapolis, Ind.: The Bobbs-Merrill Company, Inc., 1960), pp. 14–15.

440. "Thus the set of provable numbers does not coincide with the set of true numbers, since the former is definable in the language of arithmetic while the latter is not. Consequently the sets of provable sentences and true sentences do not coincide either. On the other hand, using the definition of truth we easily show that all the axioms of arithmetic are true and all the rules of proof are infallible. Hence all the provable sentences are true; therefore the converse cannot hold. Thus our final conclusion is: there are sentences formulated in the language of arithmetic that are true but cannot be proved on the basis of the axioms and rules of proof accepted in arithmetic."

From "Truth and Proof" by Alfred Tarski. Copyright © 1969 by Scientific American, Inc. All rights reserved. June, 1969, p. 76.

441. ". . . We make a senseless move when we assert, 'Another person cannot have *my* sensation.' If we were to provide a description of the sensation (e.g., 'a throbbing pain in the shoulder') it would be plainly false that another person cannot have *that*. If no description is provided, or in the offing, then we have not said anything."

Norman Malcolm, "The Privacy of Experience," in *Epistemology: New Essays in the Theory of Knowledge*, ed. by Avrum Stroll (New York: Harper & Row, Publishers, 1967), pp. 143–44.

442. "If sentence meanings are belief objects, then they are also objects of knowledge. If they are objects of knowledge, then the sentence 'Surovchak knows the meaning of the sentence "The cook has quit"' should be ambiguous. It could have either of two meanings:

Surovchak understands the sentence 'The cook has quit'.
Surovchak knows that the cook has quit.

But, the sentence is not ambiguous; clearly it has the former of these two meanings. Therefore sentence meanings are not objects of knowledge; hence not objects of belief."

> Howard Pospesel, "The Nonexistence of Propositions," *The Monist*, LIII (April, 1969), 284. Reprinted by permission of The Open Court Publishing Co., La Salle, Illinois.

443. "The needling season has opened for football Coach John McKay of the University of Southern California.

"Referring to Ohio State, the Trojans' opponent in the Rose Bowl, McKay said yesterday, 'They're supposed to be full of sophomores. But I notice in the roster they sent us they had 28 lettermen. We have 14.

" 'Now some of those lettermen have got to be juniors or seniors.' "

> "McKay Takes Verbal Punch at Buckeyes" (Associated Press), *The Miami News*, December 13, 1968, p. 3–B.

444. "Now a skill is not an act. It is therefore neither a witnessable nor an unwitnessable act."

> Gilbert Ryle, *The Concept of Mind* (New York: Barnes & Noble, Inc., 1949), p. 33. Reprinted by permission of the author, Hutchinson & Co., Ltd., and Barnes & Noble, Inc.

445. "Say there is a pro football player—let's call him Johnny Unitas —who is getting an injection of pain-killer in his bad ankle every day for practice. When Sunday comes around, he wants a double dose, right? And after the game, when it wears off, he can forget about it with a few beers.

"But with a horse, it's supposed to be different. The horse is supposed to get pain-killer help during his workouts, but when the day of the race comes up . . . go it alone.

"That's the silly part about the Kentucky Derby disqualification of Dancer's Image. The horse racing people are going to have to make up their minds what to do with the drug Butazolidin, generally certified as a pain-killer and a non-stimulant.

"They're going to have to take Butazolidin or leave it alone.

"If the horses can do without it on race day, make them do without it during the workouts. If the horses can't do without it, make it legal. It's that simple. Otherwise, in their effort to maintain a pristine image, the authorities are going to blow it all."

John Crittenden, "Butazolidin Should Be Legal—Or Banned All The Time," *The Miami News*, May 8, 1968, p. 1–C.

446. "Sandy Koufax, a pitcher of fairly recent times, was troubled by a tender limb. Like Dancer's Image, Sandy was rubbed down with hot stuff, and packed his ache in ice. Sandy took pills, even took an injection once in a while. And because he pitched brilliantly despite his tender arm, Sandy was a hero. Dancer's Image ran brilliantly despite his tender ankles . . . does that make him a bum? If it's all right for Johnny Unitas to take shots in his ankle, why should it be illegal for Dancer's Image?"

Ibid.

447. "Revelation is a communication of something which the person to whom that thing is revealed did not know before. For if I have done a thing or seen it done, it needs no revelation to tell me I have done it or seen it, nor to enable me to tell it or to write it.

"Revelation, therefore, cannot be applied to anything done upon earth, of which man himself is the actor or the witness; and, consequently, all the historical and anecdotal parts of the Bible, which is almost the whole of it, is not within the meaning and compass of the word 'revelation,' and, therefore, is not the word of God."

Thomas Paine, *The Age of Reason*, Part I (Indianapolis, Ind.: The Bobbs-Merrill Company, Inc., 1948), p. 13.

448. "It is always necessary that the means that are to accomplish any end be equal to the accomplishment of that end, or the end cannot be accomplished. It is in this that the difference between finite and infinite power and wisdom discovers itself. Man frequently fails in accomplishing his ends from a natural inability of the power to the purpose and frequently from the want of wisdom to apply power properly. But it is impossible for infinite power and wisdom to fail as man fails. The means it uses are always equal to the end; but human language, more especially as there is not a universal language, is incapable of being used as a universal means of unchangeable and uniform information, and therefore it is not the means that God uses in manifesting himself universally to man."

Ibid., p. 25.

449. ". . . I well remember, when about seven or eight years of age, hearing a sermon read by a relation of mine who was a great devotee of the [Christian] Church, upon the subject of what is called 'redemption by the death of the Son of God.' After the sermon was ended I went into the garden, and as I was going down the garden steps (for I perfectly recollect the spot), I revolted at the recollection of what I had heard, and thought to myself that it was making God Almighty act like a passionate man that killed his son when he could not revenge himself in any other way. . . . I believe . . . that any system of religion that has anything in it that shocks the mind of a child cannot be a true system."

Ibid., p. 41.

450. "The Cuban government has publicly displayed six captured invaders from Florida, all of whom said they were CIA agents, and some of whom said they had orders to assassinate Fidel Castro. . . .

". . . [It is puzzling] that such filibustering expeditions can still be operated out of Florida despite proclaimed Government policy against them. The prisoners in Havana told long stories of CIA recruitment and training in 'security houses' in Miami. Even allowing a generous discount for the fact that many Castro prisoners claim to have been CIA agents, the questions remain:

"Is it possible for these dangerous adventures to be planned in Florida without the CIA knowing about them? If the CIA does not know about them, what is wrong with its basic intelligence function? If it does know about them, why does it not attempt to stop them in accordance with the stated Government policy? And if it does not attempt to stop them, does it then encourage acts of terrorism and sabotage against Cuba?"

> "The Florida Filibusters," *St. Louis Post-Dispatch*, August 8, 1967.

451. "[There is] . . . a dilemma which must inform the views of all those who hold that truth is subjectivity. This dilemma is as follows.

"If I hold that truth is subjectivity, what status am I to give to the denial of the proposition that truth is subjectivity? If I produce arguments to refute this denial I appear committed to the view that there are criteria by appeal to which the truth about truth can be vindicated. If I refuse to produce arguments, on the grounds that there can be neither argument nor criteria in such a case, then I appear committed to the view that any view embraced with sufficient subjective passion is as warranted as any other in respect of truth, including the view that truth is not subjectivity."

> Alasdair MacIntyre, "Existentialism," in *A Critical History of Western Philosophy*, ed. by D. J. O'Connor, p. 512. Copyright © 1964 by Free Press of Glencoe, Inc.

452. "'Do you know anyone who isn't conning somebody?' asked the cynical celebrity who turned up in a charity ward in Chicago last week. The white-bearded patient was none other than ex-confidence man Joseph Weil, better known as the Yellow Kid, who billed himself in a 1948 autobiography as America's Master Swindler and boasted of hauling in $8 million in 40 years via phony stocks, crooked card games and other shady schemes. Now 93 and dead broke, the Kid was in Cook County Hospital recuperating from a broken hip and reminiscing about better days. 'I never found a man I couldn't take,' he claimed, 'and any con man knows you can't cheat an honest man. A swindling victim must have larceny in his own heart.' "

Newsweek, July 8, 1968, p. 45.

453. "A man who employs rhetoric to induce consent [on philosophical issues] and pretends to be defending his conclusions by philosophical reasoning is either a rogue or a fool. He is a fool if he believes his words have philosophical value, and he is a rogue if, knowing his methods are irrelevant to rational inquiry, he parades his silvery words in the role of serious argument."

James W. Cornman and Keith Lehrer, *Philosophical Problems and Arguments: An Introduction*, pp. 36–37. Copyright ©, The Macmillan Company, 1968.

454. "Recent advances in understanding of the minimum number of persons needed to maintain a self-sustaining human social unit provide additional evidence in favor of our view that Jabrud served as a work camp and that Shubbabiq was a base camp. William W. Howells of Harvard University has suggested that a self-sustaining group must number between 20 and 24 individuals. (He does not imply that the group would necessarily remain together during the entire year.) Taking Howells' estimate as a starting point, we can propose that any base camp where a group could live at full strength must include enough space for the daily activities of 20 to 24 people over a period of several months. Raoul Naroll of the State University of New York at Buffalo suggests that the minimum amount of sheltered space required by an individual is some 10 square meters. On this basis the 178 square meters of floor space in the Jabrud shelter could not have accommodated more than 18 individuals. Shubbabiq cave has enough sheltered floor space for 25 to 30 individuals. Taken together with the differences in the composition of the tool assemblages at the two sites, this leads us to conclude that the sites are basically different types of settlement within a differentiated settlement system."

> From "Stone Tools and Human Behavior" by Sally R. Binford and Lewis R. Binford. Copyright © 1969 by Scientific American, Inc. All rights reserved. April, 1969, p. 82.

455. ". . . The peculiar evil of silencing the expression of an opinion is, that it is robbing the human race: posterity as well as the existing generation; those who dissent from the opinion, still more than those who hold it. If the opinion is right, they are deprived of the opportunity of exchanging error for truth: if wrong, they lose, what is almost as great a benefit, the clearer perception and livelier impression of truth, produced by its collision with error."

> John Stuart Mill, *On Liberty* (Chicago: Henry Regnery Co., 1955), p. 24.

456. "A spiritual soul cannot be corrupted, since it possesses no matter; it cannot be disintegrated, since it has no substantial parts; it cannot lose its individual unity, since it is self-subsisting, nor its internal energy, since it contains within itself all the sources of its energies. The human soul cannot die. Once it exists, it cannot disappear; it will necessarily exist for ever, endure without end."

> Jacques Maritain, *The Range of Reason* (New York: Charles Scribner's Sons, 1953), p. 60. Reprinted by permission of the publisher.

457. "For years it has been an open secret that the FBI maintained a tap on the telephone calls of Dr. Martin Luther King. Last week, in a Houston courtroom, an FBI agent officially admitted that he had supervised that eavesdropping operation and that it was his 'understanding' that the taps continued until the civil-rights leader's assassination in 1968. Two other agents admitted that they had spent years of their lives plugged into the private conversations of Black Muslim leader Elijah Muhammad. In both cases it was ascertained that the taps probably had continued well past the June 30, 1965, date when President Lyndon Johnson ordered an end to wiretap cases except those authorized by the Attorney General for 'national security' reasons.

". . . The clear implication was that either the FBI had ignored LBJ's order—or that the two Negro leaders were indeed involved in some top-secret security scandal."

> "Investigations: Confessions of the FBI," *Newsweek,* June 16, 1969, pp. 29–30.

458. "Article 13. *Whether the Knowledge of God Is of Future Contingent Things?*

". . . Everything known by God must necessarily be, because even what we ourselves know must necessarily be; and, of course, the knowledge of God is much more certain than ours. But no future contingent thing must necessarily be. Therefore no contingent future thing is known by God." [186]

> St. Thomas Aquinas, *Summa Theologica,* Great Books of the Western World, Vol. XIX (Chicago: Encyclopaedia Britannica, Inc., 1952), First Part, Question 14, Article 13. Reprinted by permission of Burns & Oates Ltd. and Benziger Brothers, Inc., copyright owners.

---

[186] Aquinas states this argument but does not subscribe to it. He does subscribe to 459 and 460.

459. (Continuation of preceding passage)

"*On the contrary*, It is written (Ps. 32. 15), *He Who hath made the hearts of every one of them; Who understandeth all their works,* that is, of men. Now the works of men are contingent, since they are subject to free choice. Therefore God knows future contingent things."

Ibid.

460. (Continuation of preceding passage)

"*I answer that,* Since as was shown above (A. 9), God knows all things, not only things actual but also things in the power of Him and the creature; and since some of these are future contingent to us, it follows that God knows future contingent things."

Ibid.

461. "If a limited number of Communists with no national roots were our enemy, it would be reasonable to expect their early defeat and liquidation. This, accordingly, was predicted. 'The reports of progress,' as Senator Mansfield has said, 'are strewn like burned-out tanks all along the road which has led [us] ever more deeply into Vietnam.' And after each report of progress the American people learned that, in effect, nothing had been changed. The progress, if real, was invisible. The roots of the opposition, all too evidently, went far deeper."

> John Kenneth Galbraith, *How to Get Out of Vietnam* (New York: The New American Library, Inc., 1967), p. 27. Reprinted by permission of the author.

462. "The old conception of logic is approximately as follows: logic is the account of the most universal properties of things, the account of those properties which are common to all things; just as ornithology is the science of birds, zoology the science of all animals, biology the science of all living beings, so logic is the science of *all* things, the science of being as such. If this were the case, it would remain wholly unintelligible whence logic derives its certainty. For we surely do not know all things. We have not observed everything and hence we cannot know how everything behaves."

Hans Hahn, "Logic, Mathematics and Knowledge of Nature," trans. by Arthur Pap, in *Logical Positivism*, ed. by A. J. Ayer (New York: The Free Press, 1959), p. 152.

463. "The fetus is a separate living thing that may be aborted only if the mother's life is in danger from the child she is carrying, says orthodox rabbi Tibor H. Stern, spiritual leader of Jacob C. Cohen Community Synagogue on Miami Beach.

"'Jewish law considers the fetus life, from the moment of conception,' he says. And it is 'a separate entity, not a part of the mother' and therefore she has no personal right over the fetus, he argues.

•   •   •

"He bases his argument of life at conception on Jewish law's prohibition of work on the Sabbath, except to save a life. He says that since Jewish law rules that the delivery of a child is permissible on the Sabbath, even if the mother is already dead, this indicates that the fetus is life."

"Mother Can't Make Choice," *The Miami News*, April 17, 1969, p. 5–C.

464. "Concluding his arguments [against abortion], Rabbi Stern says:

"Jewish law permits capital punishment only for a criminal and a fetus has committed no crime."

Ibid.

465. ". . . It is untrue that all mediate deductive inferences can be expressed in syllogisms, if only because it is also untrue that all propositions can be expressed in subject-predicate form."

> J. P. Day, "John Stuart Mill," in *A Critical History of Western Philosophy*, ed. by D. J. O'Connor, p. 345. Copyright © 1964 by Free Press of Glencoe, Inc.

466. "If we assume that whenever in an assertion something is mentioned by name by a speaker, he is referring to that thing, certain very paradoxical conclusions can be deduced. It would follow that when I write in my paper 'I am not, of course, referring to Ludwig Wittgenstein', I would be referring to Ludwig Wittgenstein. But if someone were asked to show where in my paper I had referred to Ludwig Wittgenstein, it would be absurd for him to point to the statement in which I say, 'I am not referring to Ludwig Wittgenstein'. . . . [In this case] I would have used Wittgenstein's name. Therefore, to mention someone by name is not necessarily to refer to him."

> Leonard Linsky, "Reference and Referents," in *Philosophy and Ordinary Language*, ed. by Charles E. Caton (Urbana, Ill.: University of Illinois Press, 1963), p. 79.

467. "Asked if he felt the objective was important, a senior paratrooper officer commented: 'Well, it sort of commands the valley, so in a conventional war it would be important. But this isn't a conventional war, so I guess it means nothing.' "

> Peter Arnett, "Dak To Victory Empty" (Associated Press), *The News and Observer* (Raleigh, North Carolina), November 26, 1967, p. 2–I.

468. "Induction is sometimes conceived as a method that leads, by means of mechanically applicable rules, from observed facts to corresponding general principles. In this case, the rules of inductive inference would provide effective canons of scientific discovery; induction would be a mechanical procedure analogous to the familiar routine for the multiplication of integers, which leads, in a finite number of predetermined and mechanically performable steps, to the corresponding product. Actually, however, no such general and mechanical induction procedure is available at present; otherwise, the much studied problem of the causation of cancer, for example, would hardly have remained unsolved to this day."

Carl G. Hempel, *Philosophy of Natural Science* (Englewood Cliffs, N. J.: Prentice-Hall, Inc., 1966), p. 14.

469. (Continuation of preceding passage)
"Nor can the discovery of such a [general and mechanical induction] procedure ever be expected. For—to mention one reason —scientific hypotheses and theories are usually couched in terms that do not occur at all in the description of the empirical findings on which they rest, and which they serve to explain. For example, theories about the atomic and subatomic structure of matter contain terms such as 'atom', 'electron', 'proton', 'neutron', 'psi-function', etc.; yet they are based on laboratory findings about the spectra of various gases, tracks in cloud and bubble chambers, quantitative aspects of chemical reactions, and so forth—all of which can be described without the use of those "theoretical terms". Induction rules of the kind here envisaged would therefore have to provide a mechanical routine for constructing, on the basis of the given data, a hypothesis or theory stated in terms of some quite novel concepts, which are nowhere used in the description of the data themselves. Surely, no general mechanical rule of procedure can be expected to achieve this."

Ibid.

470. "Senator Thurmond's tactics yesterday in questioning Justice Fortas have no place in a civilized government. They were tactics that would only be used by the crudest policeman in the backroom of a station house. They would be unacceptable in any courtroom in the Nation yet they were used against a nominee for the Nation's highest judicial office. They are tactics the Senate ought not to permit.

"The situation was ideal, of course, for Senator Thurmond. Justice Fortas could not answer the questions he was being asked without violating his oath of office and disregarding one of the basic principles of American government. If Senator Thurmond did not know this, he merely demonstrated his own ignorance. If he did know it, he engaged in the business of slapping in the face a man whose hands were tied so he could not defend himself."

> "Senatorial Abuse," *The Washington Post*, July 19, 1968. © The Washington Post.

471. "We may . . . define a metaphysical sentence as a sentence which purports to express a genuine proposition, but does, in fact, express neither a tautology nor an empirical hypothesis. And as tautologies and empirical hypotheses form the entire class of significant [i.e., meaningful] propositions, we are justified in concluding that all metaphysical assertions are nonsensical [i.e., meaningless]."

> From *Language, Truth and Logic* by Alfred Jules Ayer, Dover Publications, Inc., New York, 1952, p. 41. Reprinted through permission of the publisher and Victor Gollancz Ltd.

472. "The third major proof of God can be stated quite simply. . . .

"Until recently, scientists talked of the law of the 'conservation of matter.' However, with the discoveries in nuclear physics, and following Madame Curie's experiments with radium, scientists have now found there *is* a certain amount of 'disintegration' in matter!

189 Arguments in Their Natural Habitat

"This *deterioration* of matter is a scientific fact! Uranium (U 238) gradually disintegrates through many intermediate stages into lead (Pb 206). Uranium, as you may well know, is radioactive and gives off energy in the form of radiation.

"Gradually, over a period of seemingly limitless years, this radioactive material disintegrates into lead! *There is no new uranium coming into existence today!*

"This means, simply stated, that science has *proved* that this earth is gradually running down! . . .

"Science has firmly established, then, *there has been no past eternity of matter!*

"Matter must have at one time COME INTO EXISTENCE! Since matter by its very nature has had no *past eternity*, it had to have been, at one time, *brought into existence!*

"*Creation,* then, the *very existence of things,* absolutely *demands* and *requires* a Creator! That which is made requires a Maker! That which is produced requires a Producer!

"Matter, it has been firmly established, has been *made*—it did not just 'happen' and has had no past eternity! Therefore the third great proof is that the *creation* requires a great *Creator!*"

Garner Ted Armstrong, *Seven Proofs God EXISTS!* (Pasadena, California: Ambassador College, 1960), pp. 2–3.

473. "'. . . I have made some inquiries myself in the last few days, but the results have, I fear, been negative. One thing only appears to be certain, and that is that Mr. James Desmond, who is the next heir, is an elderly gentleman of a very amiable disposition, so that this persecution does not arise from him. I really think that we may eliminate him entirely from our calculations.'"

Sir Arthur Conan Doyle, *The Hound of the Baskervilles* (New York: Grosset & Dunlap, Publishers, 1902), p. 75. Reprinted by permission of the Estate of Sir Arthur Conan Doyle.

474. (Continuation of preceding passage)

" '. . . There remain the people who will actually surround Sir Henry Baskerville upon the moor.'

" 'Would it not be well in the first place to get rid of this Barrymore couple?'

" 'By no means. You could not make a greater mistake. If they are innocent it would be a cruel injustice, and if they are guilty we should be giving up all chance of bringing it home to them. No, no, we will preserve them upon our list of suspects.' "

Ibid., pp. 75–76.

475. ". . . It is possible to give a quite plausible argument to support premise (4) ['A complete explanation cannot be infinitely long']. Consider that we would not call something an explanation unless we could completely express it, because the function of an explanation is to make what it explains intelligible, and something is intelligible only if it can be expressed. But a statement that is infinitely long is one that cannot ever be fully stated or expressed. Thus, no complete explanation can be infinitely long."

James W. Cornman and Keith Lehrer, *Philosophical Problems and Arguments: An Introduction,* p. 302. Copyright ©, The Macmillan Company, 1968.

476. "[There are two opposed views about the nature of scientific theories: realism and instrumentalism.] The instrumentalist interpretation of quantum theory is implied by positivism; positivism is false; hence, we must interpret quantum theory in a realistic fashion."

From a term paper for Philosophy of Science, University of Miami, August, 1969.

477. "Without the yak they [i.e., the Tibetans] could have no milk; without the milk they could have no butter; without the butter they could have no tea; without the tea they could have no existence. Selah. Without the yak they could have no plough; without the plough they could have no crop; without the crop they could have no food; without the food they could have no existence. Selah. Without the yak they could have no loads; without the loads they could have no goods; without the goods they could have no barter; without the barter they could have no existence. Selah. Without the yak they could have no wool; without the wool they could have no money; without the money they could have no goods; without the goods they could have no existence. Selah."

> George N. Patterson, *Tibetan Journey* (London: Faber & Faber, Ltd., 1954). Reprinted by permission of Faber & Faber, Ltd. and W. W. Norton & Company, Inc. American edition entitled *Journey with Loshay.*

478. "Certainly none of the substantial inferences that one comes across in the physical sciences is of a syllogistic type. This is because, in the physical sciences, we are not seriously interested in enumerating the common properties of sets of objects, but are concerned with relations of other kinds."

> Stephen Toulmin, *The Philosophy of Science: An Introduction* (New York: Harper & Row, Publishers, 1953), p. 33.

479. "As a challenge to theism, the problem of evil has traditionally been posed in the form of a dilemma: if God is perfectly loving, he must wish to abolish evil; and if he is all-powerful, he must be able to abolish evil. But evil exists; therefore God cannot be both omnipotent and perfectly loving."

> John Hick, *Philosophy of Religion* (Englewood Cliffs, N. J.: Prentice-Hall, Inc., 1963), p. 40.

480. ". . . Law-sentences in general answer to this ideal [of independence of context of utterance]; and therefore subject-predicate law-sentences answer to it. . . ."

P. F. Strawson, *Introduction to Logical Theory* (London: Methuen & Co., Ltd., 1952), p. 215.

481. "Yesterday, Rothblatt sent a message to President Nixon asking that Boyle be allowed to return to the United States until such time as he is summoned as a witness or to stand trial in the case.

"Today, in what was referred to as an 'interim reply,' the Army said Boyle had been 'flagged' as a result of charges pending against him.

"The Army reply added:

" 'In accordance with paragraph two, Army regulation 600–31, no favorable personnel action can be taken with respect to a flagged individual except as authorized by the regulation. A reassignment is a favorable personnel action.' "

" 'Army gives me medal . . . and then jail' " (The New York Times News Service), *The Miami News,* September 27, 1969, p. 10–A. © 1969 by The New York Times Company. Reprinted by permission.

482. "Liberty, or freedom, signifieth, properly, the absence of opposition; by opposition, I mean external impediments of motion; and may be applied no less to irrational, and inanimate creatures, than to rational. For whatsoever is so tied, or environed, as it cannot move but within a certain space, which space is determined by the opposition of some external body, we say it hath not liberty to go further. . . .

"And according to this proper, and generally received meaning of the word, a freeman, *is he, that in those things, which by his strength and wit he is able to do, is not hindered to do what he has a will to.* But when the words *free,* and *liberty,* are applied to any thing but bodies, they are abused; for that which is not subject to motion is not subject to impediment. . . ."

Thomas Hobbes, *Leviathan,* in *Hobbes Selections,* ed. by Frederick J. E. Woodbridge (New York: Charles Scribner's Sons, 1930), pp. 369–70. Reprinted by permission of the publisher.

483. "It is sometimes said that scientific explanations effect a reduction of a puzzling, and often unfamiliar, phenomenon to facts and principles with which we are already familiar. . . .

". . . [This thesis] does not stand up under close examination. To begin with, this view would seem to imply the idea that phenomena with which we are already familiar are not in need of, or perhaps incapable of, scientific explanation; whereas in fact, science does seek to explain such 'familiar' phenomena as the regular sequence of day and night and of the seasons, the phases of the moon, lightning and thunder, the color patterns of rainbows and of oil slicks, and the observation that coffee and milk, or white and black sand, when stirred or shaken, will mix, but never unmix again."

Carl G. Hempel, *Philosophy of Natural Science* (Englewood Cliffs, N. J.: Prentice-Hall, Inc., 1966), p. 83.

484. "Pushing aside legal stumbling blocks, U. S. Judge C. Clyde Atkins has ordered Dade County to get on with the job of desegregating its schools.

•   •   •

"While putting the weight of the federal court behind the school board's plan, Judge Atkins made it clear he feels not enough has been done, and he expects the school system to move further and faster than it has.

"He directed the School Board to bring back within 30 days a comprehensive study on the 'administrative feasibility' of complete integration of all elementary and junior high schools by January.

"The judge cited the 1968 Adams vs. Mathews case, which states: 'If in a school district there are still all-Negro schools . . . the existing plan fails to meet constitutional standards.'

"Judge Atkins said that even though the Dade School Board's plan has met with the approval of the U. S. Department of Health, Education and Welfare, it 'does not meet Constitutional standards.'"

> Ellis Berger, "School Plan Upheld Here," *The Miami News*, August 30, 1969, p. 1–A.

485. "It is now generally admitted, at any rate by philosophers, that the existence of a being having the attributes which define the god of any non-animistic religion cannot be demonstratively proved. To see that this is so, we have only to ask ourselves what are the premises from which the existence of such a god could be deduced. If the conclusion that a god exists is to be demonstratively certain, then these premises must be certain; for, as the conclusion of a deductive argument is already contained in the premises, any uncertainty there may be about the truth of the premises is necessarily shared by it. But we know that no empirical proposition can ever be anything more than probable. It is only *a priori* propositions that are logically certain. But we cannot deduce the existence of a god from an *a priori* proposition. For we know that the reason why *a priori* propositions are certain is that they are tautologies. And from a set of tautologies nothing but a further tautology can be validly deduced. It follows that there is no possibility of demonstrating the existence of a god."

> From *Language, Truth and Logic* by Alfred Jules Ayer, Dover Publications, Inc., New York, 1952, pp. 114–15. Reprinted through permission of the publisher and Victor Gollancz Ltd.

486. (Continuation of preceding passage)
"What is not so generally recognized is that there can be no

way of proving that the existence of a god, such as the God of Christianity, is even probable. Yet this also is easily shown. For if the existence of such a god were probable, then the proposition that he existed would be an empirical hypothesis. And in that case it would be possible to deduce from it, and other empirical hypotheses, certain experiential propositions which were not deducible from those other hypotheses alone. But in fact this is not possible."

Ibid., p. 115.

487. ". . . If my categories of thought determine what I observe, then what I observe provides no independent control over my thought. On the other hand, if my categories of thought do not determine what I observe, then what I observe must be uncategorized, that is to say, formless and nondescript—hence again incapable of providing any test of my thought. So in neither case is it possible for observation, be it what it may, to provide any independent control over thought." [187]

> Israel Scheffler, *Science and Subjectivity* (Indianapolis, Ind.: The Bobbs-Merrill Company, Inc., 1967), p. 13. Reprinted by permission of the author, The Bobbs-Merrill Company, Inc., and Curtis Brown, Ltd.

488. "Zsa Zsa Gabor was told in front of millions of television viewers last night she is vain, untalented and a complete nonevent. . . .

"The incident took place on a late-night celebrity program, 'The Eamonn Andrews Show.' Zsa Zsa's outspoken fellow guest was comedian Peter Cook. . . .

" 'You cannot be very talented yourself otherwise you would recognize talent in others and you would not have said I was untalented,' bit back Miss Gabor [in response to Cook's criticism]."

---

[187] Scheffler states this argument but does not subscribe to it.

"Zsa Zsa Told She's Untalented Non-Event" (Reuters News Service), *The Miami News*, January 10, 1969, p. 5–A.

489. ". . . All propositions which have factual content are empirical hypotheses; and . . . the function of an empirical hypothesis is to provide a rule for the anticipation of experience. And this means that every empirical hypothesis must be relevant to some actual, or possible, experience, so that a statement which is not relevant to any experience is not an empirical hypothesis, and accordingly has no factual content."

From *Language, Truth and Logic* by Alfred Jules Ayer, Dover Publications, Inc., New York, 1952, p. 41. Reprinted through permission of the publisher and Victor Gollancz Ltd.

490. "Every idea is deriv'd from preceding impressions; and we have no impression of self or substance, as something simple and individual. We have, therefore, no idea of them in that sense."

David Hume, *A Treatise of Human Nature* (Oxford: The Clarendon Press, 1888), p. 633.

491. "Emory says he is related to Bryan McCall (Tour 3), but not to Sam McCall (Tour 2A). When reminded that Bryan is related to Sam, he said, 'Well, then, so am I.' It takes an outsider to get these folks together on genealogy."

T. W. Reynolds, *High Lands* (n.p.: By the Author, 1964), p. 144.

492. "It has been said that once at least a higher gift than grace did flesh and blood refine, God's essence and his very self—in the body of Jesus. Whether this statement is true or false is not now the point but whether it's so obscure as to be senseless. Obscure undoubtedly it is but senseless it is not, beyond the scope of reason

it is not. For to say that in Nero God was incarnate is not to utter a senseless string of words nor merely to express a surprising sentiment; it is to make a statement which is absurd because it is against all reason. . . . The words, 'In Nero God was incarnate' are not without any meaning; one who utters them makes a statement, he makes a statement which is absurd and *against* all reason and therefore *not* beyond the scope of reason. Now if a statement is not beyond the scope of reason then any logically parallel statement is also not beyond the scope of reason. . . . The statement 'In Jesus God was incarnate' is logically parallel to 'In Nero God was incarnate.' The latter we noticed is not beyond the scope of reason. Therefore the statement 'In Jesus God was incarnate' is not beyond the scope of reason."

> John Wisdom, "The 'Logic of "God," ' " in *The Existence of God,* ed. by John Hick (New York: The Macmillan Company, 1964), pp. 295–96.

493. ". . . When are two things of the same kind? Merely to belong to some one class is not enough; for *any* two things belong to some one class."

> Nelson Goodman, *Fact, Fiction, and Forecast,* 2nd ed. (Indianapolis, Ind.: The Bobbs-Merrill Company, Inc., 1965), p. 44.

494. (Continuation of preceding passage)
"And to belong to all the same classes is far too much; for no two things belong to all the same classes."

> *Ibid.*

495. "Frazier said he told Ellis 'You're no champ. You won't fight anybody. A champ's got to fight everybody.' "

> "Liston Apparently Next for Jimmy," *The Miami News,* June 24, 1969, p. 1–C.

496. "The first form of the [referential] theory [of meaning] can easily be shown to be inadequate by virtue of the fact that two expressions can have different meanings but the same referent. Russell's classic example of this point concerns 'Sir Walter Scott' and 'the author of *Waverley*.' These two expressions refer to the same individual, since Scott is the author of *Waverley*, but they do not have the same meaning. If they did, the statement that Scott is the author of *Waverley* would be known to be true just by knowing the meaning of the constituent terms. It is a fundamental principle that whenever two referring expressions have the same meaning, for example, 'my only uncle' and 'the only brother either of my parents has,' then the identity statement with these terms as components, 'My only uncle is the only brother either of my parents has,' is necessarily true just by virtue of the meanings of these expressions. But this is not the case with 'Scott is the author of *Waverley*.' "

> William Alston, *Philosophy of Language* (Englewood Cliffs, N. J.: Prentice-Hall, Inc., 1964), p. 13.

497. ". . . Compare first the thing statement

> This is red (*P*)

and a categorical appearance statement

> Redness will be sensed. (*R*)

". . . May we say, then, that the statement *P* above entails *R*, as these statements would ordinarily be interpreted? Possibly it is obvious that no contradiction is involved in affirming *P* and denying *R*. The following considerations, however, may make the matter clearer.

"Taken in conjunction with certain *other* thing statements *Q*, referring to observation conditions, *P* does entail *R*. The following is such a statement *Q*:

This is perceived under normal conditions; and if this is red and is perceived under normal conditions, redness will be sensed. (Q)

". . . Taken in conjunction, not with Q, but with still *other* thing statements S, also referring to observation conditions, P entails not-R. An example of S would be:

This is perceived under conditions which are normal except for the presence of blue lights; and if this is red and is perceived under conditions which are normal except for the presence of blue lights, redness will not be sensed. (S)

As these statements would ordinarily be interpreted, S is logically consistent with P; there is no contradiction involved in affirming one and denying the other. But the conjunction of P and S, if it is logically consistent, must entail everything that P entails and cannot entail anything logically incompatible with what P entails. If P and S entail not-R, it is impossible that P entail R. Hence 'This is red' (P) does not entail 'Redness will be sensed' (R)."

Reprinted from Roderick M. Chisholm: *Perceiving: A Philosophical Study*, pp. 191–92. © 1957 by Cornell University. Used by permission of Cornell University Press.

498. "The bigger the burger the better the burger. The burgers are bigger at Burger King."

Jingle from a television commercial.

499. ". . . If I wish to refute a philosophical opponent . . . I try to prove that his definitions involve a contradiction. Suppose, for example, that he is maintaining that 'A is a free agent' is equivalent to 'A's actions are uncaused.' Then I refute him by getting him to admit that 'A is a free agent' is entailed by 'A is morally responsible for his actions' whereas 'A's actions are uncaused' entails 'A is not morally responsible for his actions.' "

From *Language, Truth and Logic* by Alfred Jules Ayer, Dover Publications, Inc., New York, 1952, p. 70, n. 2. Reprinted through permission of the publisher and Victor Gollancz Ltd.

500. ". . . There is an evident absurdity in pretending to demonstrate a matter of fact, or to prove it by any arguments *a priori*. Nothing is demonstrable unless the contrary implies a contradiction. Nothing that is distinctly conceivable implies a contradiction. Whatever we conceive as existent, we can also conceive as nonexistent. There is no being, therefore, whose non-existence implies a contradiction. Consequently there is no being whose existence is demonstrable. I propose this argument as entirely decisive, and am willing to rest the whole controversy upon it."

David Hume, *Dialogues Concerning Natural Religion* (New York: Hafner Publishing Co., Inc., 1951), p. 58.

Bibliography
and Name
Index

Numerals enclosed within brackets refer to arguments in this volume.

Alsop, Stewart, "Nixon and the New Bourgeoisie," *Newsweek,* January 27, 1969, p. 96. [399, 400]

Alston, William, *Philosophy of Language.* Englewood Cliffs, N. J.: Prentice-Hall, Inc., 1964. [108, 121, 252, 253, 426, 496]

Aquinas, St. Thomas, *Summa Theologica.* Great Books of the Western World, XIX. Chicago: Encyclopaedia Britannica, Inc., 1952. [143, 330, 458–460]

Armstrong, Garner Ted, *Seven Proofs God EXISTS!* Pasadena, California: Ambassador College, 1960. [472]

Arnett, Peter, "Dak To Victory Empty" (Associated Press), *The News and Observer* (Raleigh, North Carolina), November 26, 1967, p. 2–I. [467]

Ayer, Alfred Jules, *Language, Truth and Logic.* New York: Dover Publications, Inc., 1952. [85, 233, 278, 361, 434, 471, 485, 486, 489, 499]

Barker, Stephen F., *Philosophy of Mathematics.* Englewood Cliffs, N. J.: Prentice-Hall, Inc., 1964. [232]

Barnes, Winston H. F., "The Myth of Sense-Data," *Proceedings of the Aristotelian Society,* XLV (1944–45), 89–117. [149]

Bartlett, John, *Familiar Quotations* (13th ed.). Boston: Little, Brown and Company, 1955. [378]

Benn, S. I., and R. S. Peters, *Social Principles and the Democratic State.* London: George Allen & Unwin, Ltd., 1959. [189]

Berger, Ellis, "School Plan Upheld Here," *The Miami News,* August 30, 1969, p. 1–A. [484]

Berkeley, George, *A Treatise Concerning the Principles of Human Knowledge.* Indianapolis, Ind.: The Bobbs-Merrill Company, Inc., 1957. [15, 57, 237–239, 301, 368]

The Bible. Revised Standard Version. New York: Thomas Nelson & Sons, 1952. [91, 206, 356, 425]

Binford, Sally R., and Lewis R. Binford, "Stone Tools and Human Behavior," *Scientific American,* CCXX (April, 1969), 70–84. [454]

Broad, C. D., *Five Types of Ethical Theory.* London: Routledge & Kegan Paul, Ltd., 1930. [424]

Butterfield, Herbert, *The Origins of Modern Science.* New York: The Free Press, 1957. [81, 140, 305, 306]

Campbell, C. A., "Is 'Free Will' a Pseudo-Problem?" *Mind,* LX (1951), 441–65. [429]

Carlson, A. J., *The Control of Hunger in Health and Disease.* Chicago: The University of Chicago Press, 1916. [145]

Carnap, Rudolf, "Testability and Meaning," in *Readings in the Philosophy of Science,* eds. Herbert Feigl and May Brodbeck. New York: Appleton-Century-Crofts, 1953. [383]

Cartwright, Richard, "Negative Existentials," *The Journal of Philosophy,* LVII (1960), 629–39. [113]

Caws, Peter, *The Philosophy of Science.* Princeton, N. J.: D. Van Nostrand Co., Inc., 1965. [102, 347]

Chisholm, Roderick, *Perceiving: A Philosophical Study.* Ithaca, N. Y.: Cornell University Press, 1957. [497]

Cornford, Francis M., *Plato's Theory of Knowledge.* Indianapolis, Ind.: The Bobbs-Merrill Company, Inc., 1957. [322]

Cornman, James W., and Keith Lehrer, *Philosophical Problems and Arguments: An Introduction.* New York: The Macmillan Company, 1968. [186, 308, 401, 423, 453, 475]

Crittenden, John, "Butazolidin Should Be Legal—Or Banned All The Time," *The Miami News*, May 8, 1968, p. 1–C. [445, 446]

Day, J. P., "John Stuart Mill," in *A Critical History of Western Philosophy*, ed. D. J. O'Connor. New York: The Free Press, 1964. [58, 465]

Descartes, Réné, *Meditations on First Philosophy*. Indianapolis, Ind.: The Bobbs-Merrill Company, Inc., 1960. [99, 319, 439]

Doyle, A. Conan, *The Hound of the Baskervilles*. New York: Grosset & Dunlap, Inc., 1902. [473, 474]

Edwards, Clive A., "Soil Pollutants and Soil Animals," *Scientific American*, CCXX (April, 1969), 88–99. [397, 398]

Euclid, *The Thirteen Books of Euclid's Elements*, trans. by Sir Thomas L. Heath, 3 vols. New York: Dover Publications, Inc., 1956. [337]

Ewing, A. C., *The Fundamental Questions of Philosophy*. New York: Collier Books, 1962. [243]

Faris, J. A., *Truth-Functional Logic*. New York: Free Press of Glencoe, Inc., 1962. [312]

Fitch, Frederic, "The Reality of Propositions," *The Review of Metaphysics*, IX (1955), 3–13. [196, 289]

Flew, Antony, "Theology and Falsification," in *New Essays in Philosophical Theology*, eds. Antony Flew and Alasdair MacIntyre. London: Student Christian Movement Press, 1955. [219]

Frege, Gottlob, "The Thought: A Logical Inquiry," trans. by A. M. and Marcelle Quinton, *Mind*, LXV (1956), 289–311. [230]

Galbraith, John Kenneth, *How to Get Out of Vietnam*. New York: The New American Library, Inc., 1967. [461]

Goodman, Nelson, "Art and Inquiry," *Proceedings and Addresses of the American Philosophical Association*, XLI (1968), 5–19. [213]

———, *Fact, Fiction, and Forecast* (2nd ed.). Indianapolis, Ind.: The Bobbs-Merrill Company, Inc., 1965. [244, 318, 493, 494]

———, *Languages of Art*. Indianapolis, Ind.: The Bobbs-Merrill Company, Inc., 1968. [295]

Hahn, Hans, "Logic, Mathematics and Knowledge of Nature," trans. by Arthur Pap, in *Logical Positivism*, ed. A. J. Ayer. New York: The Free Press, 1959. [462]

Hempel, Carl G., *Fundamentals of Concept Formation in Empirical*

Science. International Encyclopedia of Unified Science, II, No. 7. Chicago: The University of Chicago Press, 1952. [384]

————, *Philosophy of Natural Science.* Englewood Cliffs, N. J.: Prentice-Hall, Inc., 1966. [89, 126, 468, 469, 483]

Hick, John, ed., *The Existence of God.* New York: The Macmillan Company, 1964. [143, 156, 157, 330, 492]

————, *Philosophy of Religion.* Englewood Cliffs, N. J.: Prentice-Hall, Inc., 1963. [26, 83, 479]

————, "Theology and Verification," *Theology Today,* XVII (1960), 12–31. [220, 221]

Hobbes, Thomas, *Hobbes Selections,* ed. Frederick J. E. Woodbridge. New York: Charles Scribner's Sons, 1930. [482]

————, *Leviathan.* Chicago: Henry Regnery Co., 1956. [223, 274, 275, 406]

Hobson, Dick, "Clark Kent, After All, Can Turn into Superman," *TV Guide,* October 12, 1968, pp. 44–49. [431]

Hospers, John, "What Means This Freedom?" in *Determinism and Freedom in the Age of Modern Science,* ed. Sidney Hook. New York: Collier Books, 1961. [334]

Hume, David, *Dialogues Concerning Natural Religion.* New York: Hafner Publishing Company, Inc., 1951. [500]

————, *An Inquiry Concerning Human Understanding.* Indianapolis, Ind.: The Bobbs-Merrill Company, Inc., 1955. [139, 331]

————, *A Treatise of Human Nature.* Oxford: The Clarendon Press, 1888. [490]

James, William, "The Dilemma of Determinism," in *Essays in Pragmatism,* ed. Alburey Castell. New York: Hafner Publishing Co., Inc., 1948. [172, 297]

————, "The Sentiment of Rationality," in *Essays in Pragmatism,* ed. Alburey Castell. New York: Hafner Publishing Co., Inc., 1948. [297]

Kallman, Franz J., *Heredity in Health and Mental Disorder.* New York: W. W. Norton & Company, Inc., 1953. [128]

Kant, Immanuel, *Critique of Pure Reason.* New York: St. Martin's Press, Inc., 1961. [159, 234]

————, *Foundations of the Metaphysics of Morals.* Indianapolis, Ind.: The Bobbs-Merrill Company, Inc., 1959. [23, 142, 207]

Kelly, Herb, *The Miami News,* July 24, 1968, p. 5–B. [402]

King, Martin Luther, Jr., "Letter from Birmingham City Jail," *The New Leader,* June 24, 1963, pp. 3–11. [396]

Landers, Ann, "Dear Ann" (Publishers-Hall Syndicate), *Atlanta Journal,* June 20, 1969, p. 6–B. [437, 438]

Leibniz, Gottfried, *Leibniz Selections,* ed. Philip P. Wiener. New York: Charles Scribner's Sons, 1951. [303, 395]

Lemmon, E. J., *Beginning Logic.* London: Thomas Nelson and Sons Ltd., 1965. [355]

Linsky, Leonard, "Reference and Referents," in *Philosophy and Ordinary Language,* ed. Charles E. Caton. Urbana, Ill.: University of Illinois Press, 1963. [466]

————, *Referring.* London: Routledge & Kegan Paul, Ltd., 1967. [339]

Lipsyte, Robert, "Logic Ends When It's Wilt Vs. Russell" (*New York Times* column), *The Miami News,* April 28, 1969, p. 3–B. [185]

Locke, John, *An Essay Concerning Human Understanding,* 2 vols. New York: Dover Publications, Inc., 1959. [115, 212]

MacIntyre, Alasdair, "Existentialism," in *A Critical History of Western Philosophy,* ed. D. J. O'Connor. New York: The Free Press, 1964. [451]

Malcolm, Norman, "[Abstract of] Scientific Materialism and the Identity Theory," *The Journal of Philosophy,* LX (Oct. 24, 1963), 662–63. [96]

————, "Anselm's Ontological Arguments," *The Philosophical Review,* LXIX (1960), 41–62. [158]

————, "The Privacy of Experience," in *Epistemology: New Essays in the Theory of Knowledge,* ed. Avrum Stroll. New York: Harper & Row, Publishers, 1967. [79, 441]

Maritain, Jacques, *The Range of Reason.* New York: Charles Scribner's Sons, 1953. [456]

Mill, John Stuart, *On Liberty.* Chicago: Henry Regnery Co., 1955. [455]

————, *A System of Logic, Rationative and Inductive.* New York: Harper & Brothers, Publishers, 1859. [232]

Moore, George Edward, *Some Main Problems of Philosophy.* London: George Allen & Unwin, Ltd., 1953. [408]

Newman, H. H., F. N. Freeman, and K. J. Holzinger, *Twins: A Study of Heredity and Environment.* Chicago: University of Chicago Press, 1937. [88]

Oliver, James Willard, "Formal Fallacies and Other Invalid Arguments," *Mind,* LXXVI (1967), 463–78. [203, 209]

Paine, Thomas, *The Age of Reason,* Part I. Indianapolis, Ind.: The Bobbs-Merrill Company, Inc., 1948. [447–449]

Pap, Arthur, *An Introduction to the Philosophy of Science.* New York: Free Press of Glencoe, Inc., 1962. [41]

Pascal, Blaise, *Pensées.* New York: Modern Library, Inc., 1941. [103]

Patterson, George N., *Tibetan Journey.* London: Faber & Faber, Ltd., 1954. [477]

Pearson, Karl, "On the Laws of Inheritance of Man," *Biometrika,* III (1904), 131–90. [166]

Pitcher, George, *The Philosophy of Wittgenstein.* Englewood Cliffs, N. J.: Prentice-Hall, Inc., 1964. [242]

Place, U. T., "Is Consciousness a Brain Process?" *British Journal of Psychology,* XLVII (1956), 44–50. [94]

Plato, *The Dialogues of Plato,* trans. by B. Jowett. 2 vols. New York: Random House, 1892. [131, 132, 322, 326, 345, 430]

Popper, Karl, "Why Are the Calculi of Logic and Arithmetic Applicable to Reality?" in *Conjectures and Refutations.* New York: Basic Books, Inc., Publishers, 1962. [55]

Pospesel, Howard, "The Nonexistence of Propositions," *The Monist,* LIII (April, 1969), 280–92. [442]

Quine, W. V., *Mathematical Logic,* rev. ed. Cambridge, Mass.: Harvard University Press, 1958. [40]

———, "Paradox," *Scientific American,* CCVI (April, 1962), 84–96. [176, 320]

Reynolds, T. W., *High Lands.* N.p.: By the author, 1964. [491]

Rosenzweig, Mark R., "The Mechanisms of Hunger and Thirst," in *Psychology in the Making,* ed. Leo Postman. New York: Alfred A. Knopf, Inc., 1962. [145–147]

Roux, Joanny, "La Faim, Étude Physio-psychologique," *Bulletin de la Société d'Anthropologie de Lyon*, XVI (1897), 409–55. [146]

Russell, Bertrand, *A History of Western Philosophy*. New York: Simon and Schuster, Inc., 1945. [20, 27]

——, *My Philosophical Development*. New York: Simon and Schuster, Inc., 1959. [432]

——, *The Principles of Mathematics*. London: George Allen & Unwin, Ltd., 1903. [113]

Ryle, Gilbert, *The Concept of Mind*. New York: Barnes & Noble, Inc., 1949. [420, 444]

——, "The Theory of Meaning," in *British Philosophy in the Mid-Century*, ed. C. A. Mace. London: George Allen & Unwin, Ltd., 1957. [176, 276, 283, 321]

Salmon, Wesley C., *The Foundations of Scientific Inference*. Pittsburgh: University of Pittsburgh Press, 1967. [119, 194, 328, 336]

Scheffler, Israel, *Conditions of Knowledge: An Introduction to Epistemology and Education*. Glenview, Ill.: Scott, Foresman & Company, 1965. [418]

——, *Science and Subjectivity*. Indianapolis, Ind.: The Bobbs-Merrill Company, Inc., 1967. [487]

Shannon, Claude, "A Symbolic Analysis of Relay and Switching Circuits," *Transactions of the American Institute of Electrical Engineers*, LVII (1938), 713–23. [178, 179]

Skyrms, Brian, *Choice and Chance: An Introduction to Inductive Logic*. Belmont, California: Dickenson Publishing Company, Inc., 1966. [262]

Spinoza, Benedict de, *The Chief Works of Benedict de Spinoza*, trans. by R. H. M. Elwes. 2 vols. New York: Dover Publications, Inc., 1951. [375]

Strawson, P. F., *Introduction to Logical Theory*. London: Methuen & Co., Ltd., 1952. [339, 480]

Tarski, Alfred, "Truth and Proof," *Scientific American*, CCXX (June, 1969), 63–77. [440]

Terrell, D. B., and Robert Baker, *Exercises in Logic*. New York: Holt, Rinehart & Winston, Inc., 1967. [270]

Toulmin, Stephen, *The Philosophy of Science: An Introduction*. New York: Harper & Row, Publishers, 1953. [478]

Turing, A. M., "Computing Machinery and Intelligence," *Mind*, LIX (1950), 433–60. [3]

Urmson, J. O., *Philosophical Analysis: Its Development Between the Two World Wars*. Oxford: The Clarendon Press, 1956. [404]

Van Buren, Abigail, "Dear Abby" (Chicago Tribune–New York News Syndicate, Inc.), *The Miami News*, April 21, 1969, p. 8–B. [436]

————, "Dear Abby" (Chicago Tribune–New York News Syndicate, Inc.), *The Miami News*, August 14, 1969, p. 22–D. [435]

Von Braun, Wernher, "Science Is Helping to Put Face on God," *The Miami News*, August 6, 1966, p. 4–A. [427, 428]

Waley, Arthur, *Three Ways of Thought in Ancient China*. Garden City, N.Y.: Doubleday & Company, Inc., 1956. [136, 222]

Watling, J. L., "Descartes," in *A Critical History of Western Philosophy*, ed. D. J. O'Connor. New York: The Free Press, 1964. [25]

Westphal, Fred A., *The Activity of Philosophy: A Concise Introduction*. Englewood Cliffs, N. J.: Prentice-Hall, Inc., 1969. [149]

Wilcox, Bob, "Keeping Kosher: A Serious Matter," *The Miami News*, January 15, 1970, p. 7–C. [407]

Windelband, Wilhelm, *A History of Philosophy*, 2 vols. New York: Harper & Brothers, Publishers, 1958. [36]

Wisdom, John, "The 'Logic of "God," ' " in *The Existence of God*, ed. John Hick. New York: The Macmillan Company, 1964. [492]

Wittgenstein, Ludwig, *Philosophical Investigations*. New York: The Macmillan Company, 1953. [50, 62]

Wylie, C. R., Jr., *101 Puzzles in Thought and Logic*. New York: Dover Publications, Inc., 1957. [105, 170]